FAITH OF THE FATHERS

FAITH OF THE FATHERS

Religion and matters of faith contained in the Presidents' Inaugural Addresses from George Washington to Bill Clinton.

EDITED WITH NOTES BY
J. Michael Sharman, J.D.

For permission, please write to:

Victory Publishing
114 North West Street
Culpeper, Virginia 22701

FIRST PRINTING, 1995

PRINTED IN THE UNITED STATES OF AMERICA
Library of Congress Catalog Card Number 95-90886

Dedication

This book is dedicated to my wife, Nancy. Thank you for listening to all my exclamations of wonder at the tidbits of history found in dusty old tomes. Thank you especially for continually encouraging me when you would probably have really preferred that I was doing something other than fussing with this book.

"The prophets of evil were not the builders of the Republic, nor in its crises since have they saved or served it. The faith of the fathers was a mighty force in its creation, and the faith of their descendants has wrought its progress and furnished it defenders."

William McKinley,
second inaugural address,
March 4th, 1901

"This matter is by the decree of the watchers, and the demand by the word of the holy ones: to the intent that the living may know that the most High ruleth in the kingdom of men, and giveth it to whomsoever he will, and setteth up over it the basest of men."

Daniel 4:17 (KJV)

FOREWARD

From 1789 to 1996, our Nation has had forty-one different men[1] serve as presidents. These men are as different as -- well, as different as George Washington is from Bill Clinton, but each one of them acknowledged in public addresses that they were simply leaders of a government who were under the Authority of the Ruler of All Nations. All of the men who gave inaugural addresses made that acknowledgment in their inaugural speech.

Perhaps they made the acknowledgment with the utmost piety and sincerity, perhaps only with political acumen and a cynical desire to please the people. We have had men serve as President who were beyond reproach and we have had others whose lack of character or morals often became a public problem for themselves and the nation. As John Quincy Adams said at his own inauguration, "From evil -- physical, moral, and political -- it is not our claim to be exempt." Regardless of their own adherence to each of God's laws, the acknowledgment was made that there was One who was more sovereign than they and that One was the God of our Fathers, the God of the Bible.

If all the documents which prove our nation's Christian heritage were put in your local library, there would be no remaining space left on the shelves for any other books. In this slim volume, however, is contained the proof that from the time of the consolidation of the thirteen colonies into a single nation to the present day, regardless of which person or party was in power, our nation and its chief executive officers have always recognized that we are, indeed, one nation under God. Sometimes the acknowledgment of God's sovereignty was brief and sometimes lengthy, but the inescapable fact is that throughout our nation's history, that acknowledgment was always made.

This book is not an attempt to re-publish the entire inaugural addresses of the presidents, rather it is an attempt to highlight our Christian heritage as revealed in portions of those inaugural addresses. Accordingly, all the sections of a president's inaugural address other than those which deal with religion or matters of faith will be deleted. The purpose of this book is not to give an overview of all of American history, but rather to give a speaker, scholar or researcher a reference tool to quickly find out what a president said in their inaugural address, their first official act, about God's relationship to our country.

---

[1] According to a ruling by the State Department, Grover Cleveland is both the 22nd and 24th president, because his two terms were not consecutive, even though he was only the 22nd individual to hold the office of president.

How To Use This Book

This book is a research tool, not a novel, and it has been written with the objective of allowing you to obtain the information as quickly and concisely as possible.

With rare exception, the only part of a President's inaugural address which is re-printed here is that part which dealt with religion or matters of faith. The ellipsis grammar symbol of a series of three periods (...) indicates an omission of something within the address which dealt with matters other than religion or matters of faith.

In the presidential biographies, abbreviations were used for birth (b.), death (d.), and marriage (m.). If a piece of information is omitted from a president's biographical data which was provided for other presidents (for example, "Church Service" or "Bible Used"), this omission indicates that information on that topic was not able to be found.

On matters of education, the term "homeschooled" is used to mean that while a child, the future president was taught at home under the direction of his parents in other than a classroom setting. The parents may have provided the actual instruction or the means to the instruction in the form of books or tutors, but the key point in deciding to use the term "homeschooled" was whether or not the children received schooling at home under the parents' authority. Two exceptions to this are Millard Fillmore and Andrew Johnson who were not educated on any scholastic item by anyone as children but as adults they received home instruction from their wives.

Under the term "College", the phrase "read for the law" is often seen for many of the Presidents prior to the 20th Century. The phrase "read for the law" means that the person prepared for a future career as an attorney, and for passage of the bar examination, by self-study rather than by attending law school. The course of self-study might have been under the direction of an established attorney or it might simply have been upon the student's own direction and decision of what to study. All those who studied the law prior to the 20th Century would have studied Blackstone's, <u>Commentaries on the Laws of England</u>. Those who read for the law would have been particularly dependent upon Blackstone to provide for them the basic interpretive framework upon which to hang the rest of their legal learning. In his Commentaries Blackstone said, "These laws laid down by God are the eternal immutable laws of good and evil.... This law of nature dictated by God himself, is of course superior in obligation to any other. It is binding over all the globe, in all countries, and at all times: no human laws are of any validity if contrary to this."

Table of Contents

EXECUTIVE OATH OF OFFICE

"I do solemnly swear (or affirm) that I will faithfully execute the office of President of the United States, and will to the best of my ability, preserve, protect and defend the Constitution of the United States."

United States Constitution,
Article II, Section 1, Clause 8.

GEORGE WASHINGTON
(Nonpartisan) First President

b. February 22, 1732, Pope's Creek, Westmoreland Co., Va.

d. 67 years old, December 14, 1799 at Mt. Vernon of complications after getting a cold while riding over his estates.

m. Martha Dandridge Custis Washington on January 6, 1759, a widow. They had no children together.

President: From April 30, 1789 to March 4, 1797.

Father: Augustine Washington, a planter, died when he was eleven.

Prep. School: Essentially home schooled or taught with assistance from a few tutors.

College: None.

Profession: Surveyor; Farmer; Soldier.

Denomination: Episcopal/Anglican.

Church Service: Vestryman.

Military Service: Appointed as an adjutant in the militia at age 20; Officer in Virginia Militia under Braddock; later Commander-in-Chief, Continental Army.

First Inaugural Address: Given in New York City on April 30, 1789 at the Senate Chamber at Federal Hall on Wall Street. At his request, after his first inauguration Congress adjourned to St. Paul's where divine services were held to ask for the blessing of God on the nation under its new leader.

Sworn in by: The Chancellor of New York, fellow Freemason Robert R. Livingston.

Bible used: The Bible which belonged to New York's St. John's Masonic Lodge.

Washington's Second Inaugural Address: Monday, March 4, 1793 sworn in by Associate Justice of the Supreme Court William Cushing, Senate Chamber, Congress Hall in Philadelphia. He gave the shortest inaugural address ever given: 135 words, 2 paragraphs.

Noteworthy: He began the tradition of serving a maximum of two-terms as president. Washington was the only president ever elected with a unanimous electoral vote.

Washington is frequently given the party identification as a Federalist, but he himself was adamantly non-partisan and obviously needed no party affiliation.

GEORGE WASHINGTON
FIRST INAUGURAL ADDRESS IN THE CITY OF NEW YORK
THURSDAY, APRIL 30, 1789

Washington's inaugural marked the occasion of the first freely elected leader of a democratic nation in the world's history. He knew that his peaceful passage into power would be observed by the other world governments and by "posterity".

...[I]t would be peculiarly improper to omit in this first official act my fervent supplications to that Almighty Being who rules over the universe, who presides in the councils of nations, and whose providential aids can supply every human defect, that His benediction may consecrate to the liberties and happiness of the people of the United States a Government instituted by themselves for these essential purposes, and may enable every instrument employed in its administration to execute with success the functions allotted to his charge. In tendering this homage to the Great Author of every public and private good, I assure myself that it expresses your sentiments not less than my own, nor those of my fellow-citizens at large less than either. No people can be bound to acknowledge and adore the Invisible Hand which conducts the affairs of men more than those of the United States. Every step by which they have advanced to the character of an independent nation seems to have been distinguished by some token of providential agency; and in the important revolution just accomplished in the system of their united government the tranquil deliberations and voluntary consent of so many distinct communities from which the event has resulted can not be compared with the means by which most governments have been established without some return of pious gratitude, along with an humble anticipation of the future blessings which the past seem to presage. These reflections, arising out of the present crisis, have forced themselves too strongly on my mind to be suppressed. You will join with me, I trust, in thinking that there are none under the influence of which the proceedings of a new and free government can more auspiciously commence.

...[T]here is no truth more thoroughly established than that there exists in the economy and course of nature an indissoluble union between virtue and happiness; between duty and advantage; between the genuine maxims of an honest and magnanimous policy and the solid rewards of public prosperity and felicity; since we ought to be no less persuaded that the propitious smiles of Heaven can never be expected on a nation that disregards the eternal rules of order and right which Heaven itself has ordained; and since the preservation of the sacred fire of liberty and the destiny of the republican model of government are justly considered, perhaps, as deeply, as finally, staked on the experiment entrusted to the hands of the American people.

...I shall take my present leave; but not without resorting once more to the benign Parent of the Human Race in humble supplication that, since He has been pleased to favor the American people with opportunituties for deliberating in perfect tranquillity, and dispositions for deciding with unparalleled unanimity on a form of government for the security of their union and the advancement of their happiness, so His divine blessing may be equally conspicuous in the enlarged views, the temperate consultations, and the wise measures on which the success of this Government must depend.

GEORGE WASHINGTON
SECOND INAUGURAL ADDRESS
MONDAY, MARCH 4, 1793

George Washington gave his second inaugural address on Monday, March 4, 1793 in the Senate Chamber of Congress Hall in Philadelphia. He made the shortest inaugural speech ever given, only two paragraphs containing 135 words. The main thrust of his short speech was his request to be held legally and morally accountable for any misuse of the power given to him by the People, a revolutionary concept indeed.

Fellow Citizens:

I am again called upon by the voice of my country to execute the functions of its Chief Magistrate. When the occasion proper for it shall arrive, I shall endeavor to express the high sense I entertain of this distinguished honor, and of the confidence which has been reposed in me by the people of united America.

Previous to the execution of any official act of the President the Constitution requires an oath of office. This oath I am now about to take, and in your presence: That if it shall be found during my administration of the Government I have in any instance violated willingly or knowingly the injunctions thereof, I may (besides incurring constitutional punishment) be subject to the upbraidings of all who are now witnesses of the present solemn ceremony.

JOHN ADAMS
(Federalist) Second President

b. October 19, 1735, Braintree (Quincy), Massachusetts.

d. July 4th, 1826, age 90, Braintree (Quincy), Massachusetts (50th Anniversary of the Declaration of Independence. Adams died a few hours after Jefferson.)

m. October 25, 1764 to Abigail Smith, daughter of Rev. Wm. Smith. Two daughters, 3 sons.

President from: Saturday, March 4, 1797 to -March 4th, 1801.

Father: John Adams, farmer.

Prep School: Partly at the public grammar school and partly at a private academy under Mr. Joseph Marsh.

College: Graduated from Harvard University with high honors in 1755, later got M.A. from Harvard 1758.

Military Service: None.

Profession: School teacher; lawyer; statesman.

Denomination: First Congregational Church was where he attended and was buried.

Church Service: He considered the ministry as a profession, but finally turned to the law.

Bar Membership: 1758 (Boston), 1761 (Mass. Superior Ct.).

Inaugural address given on: Saturday, March 4, 1797 at the Hall of the House of Representatives in Federal Hall, Philadelphia.

Sworn in by: Chief Justice Oliver Ellsworth.

Noteworthy: He was the first U.S. Vice-President; the first president to take up residence in the White House; and he lived longer than any other surviving president.

His integrity and love of justice is exemplified by his legal representation of the British soldiers who had, under orders, killed citizens in the "Boston Massacre." He represented them because even though he was an ardent revolutionary, he also believed everyone was entitled to a fair trial and no other lawyer would take the case.

JOHN ADAMS
INAUGURAL ADDRESS IN THE CITY OF PHILADELPHIA
SATURDAY, MARCH 4, 1797

An awkward reality of early American politics was that the "runner-up" in the presidential election became the Vice President. Adams and Jefferson fought a heated battle during the campaign and now Adams was inaugurated as President and Jefferson, the loser in the contest, was inaugurated as Adams' Vice President.

...Relying on the purity of their intentions, the justice of their cause, and the integrity and intelligence of the people, under an overruling Providence which had so signally protected this country from the first, the representatives of this nation, then consisting of little more than half its present number, not only broke to pieces the chains which were forging and the rod of iron that was lifted up, but frankly cut asunder the ties which had bound them, and launched into an ocean of uncertainty.

...[I]f elevated ideas of the high destinies of this country and of my won duties toward it, founded on a knowledge of the moral principles and intellectual improvements of the people deeply engraven on my mind in early life, and not obscured but exalted by experience and age; and, with humble reverence, I feel it to be my duty to add, if a veneration for the religion of a people who profess and call themselves Christians, and a fixed resolution to consider a decent respect for Christians among the best recommendations for the public service, can enable me in any degree to comply with your wishes, it shall be my strenuous endeavor that this sagacious injunction of the two Houses shall not be without effect.

...And may that Being who is supreme over all, the Patron of Order, the Fountain of Justice, and the Protector in all ages of the world of virtuous liberty, continue His blessing upon this nation and its Government and give it all possible success and duration consistent with the ends of His providence.

THOMAS JEFFERSON
(Republican) Third President

b. April 13, 1743, Shadwell, in Goochland (now Albemarle) Co. Va..

d. July 4th, 1826 (50th Anniversary of the Declaration of Independence. Jefferson died a few hours before Adams).

m. 1772, Martha Wayles Skelton Jefferson, a widow, one son, five daughters.

Father: Peter Jefferson, a Welsh civil engineer, Pioneer-farmer, vestryman at his church, justice of the peace. Died when Jefferson was 14.

President from: March 1, 1801 to March 4, 1809.

Jefferson and Aaron Burr both had 73 electoral votes, sending it to the House of Representatives, which chose Jefferson as President.

Prep. School: Basically home taught with private tutors.

College: Began at William and Mary in 1760 at 17 years old; graduated 1762; studied law under George Wythe.

Bar Membership: 1767, Virginia.

Profession: Attorney; Farmer; Statesman.

Denomination: Unitarian by his own statement but Episcopalian by tradition and attendance.

Church Service: Wrote a book called "The Life and Morals of Jesus of Nazareth"; he wrote Charles Thompson and said "it is a document in proof that I am a real Christian, that is to say, a disciple of the doctrines of Jesus."

Military Service: None.

Inaugural address given on: Wednesday, March 4, 1801 at the U.S. Capitol, Washington, D.C.

Sworn in by: He was the first president sworn in by Chief Justice John Marshall (who had been appointed by John Adams the night before).

Second Inaugural: Monday, March 4, 1805.

Elected with 162 of 176 electoral votes.

Sworn in by Chief Justice John Marshall at the Senate Chamber at U.S. Capitol.

Noteworthy: Although he began public service as one of the wealthiest men in America, he became so hopelessly in debt that he was forced to sell his cherished library to the Government, creating the foundation for the Library of Congress.

He was the first President inaugurated at the U.S. Capitol in what was first called Federal City and later named Washington, District of Columbia.

THOMAS JEFFERSON
FIRST INAUGURAL ADDRESS
WEDNESDAY, MARCH 4, 1801

The outcome of the election of 1800 had been in doubt until late February because Thomas Jefferson and Aaron Burr, the two leading candidates, each had received 73 electoral votes. Consequently, the House of Representatives met in a special session to resolve the impasse, pursuant to the terms spelled out in the Constitution. After 30 hours of debate and balloting, Mr. Jefferson emerged as the President. President John Adams, who had run unsuccessfully for a second term, left Washington, D.C. on the day of the inauguration to avoid attending the ceremony.

...[E]nlightened by a benign religion, professed, indeed, and practiced in various forms, yet all of them inculcating honesty, truth, temperance, gratitude, and the love of man; acknowledging and adoring an overruling Providence, which by all its dispensations proves that it delights in the happiness of man here and his greater happiness hereafter - with all these blessings, what more is necessary to make us a happy and a prosperous people? Still one thing more, fellow-citizens--a wise and frugal Government, which shall restrain men from injuring one another, shall leave them otherwise free to regulate their own pursuits of industry and improvement, and shall not take from the mouth of labor the bread it has earned. This is the sum of good government, and this is necessary to close the circle of our felicities.

...[M]ay that Infinite Power which rules the destinies of the universe lead our councils to what is best, and give them a favorable issue for your peace and prosperity.

THOMAS JEFFERSON
SECOND INAUGURAL ADDRESS
MONDAY, MARCH 4, 1805

The second inauguration of Mr. Jefferson followed an election under which the offices of President and Vice President were to be separately sought, pursuant to the newly adopted 12th Amendment to the Constitution. Jefferson's mention of the Indians -- the "Aboriginal inhabitants" -- is noteworthy because he had been spending a half hour each evening translating Christ's words in Scripture into a book entitled "The Life and Morals of Jesus of Nazareth", a book he proposed for Congress to distribute to the Indians.

In matters of religion I have considered that its free exercise is placed by the Constitution independent of the powers of the General Government. I have therefore undertaken on no occasion to prescribe the religious exercises suited to it, but have left them, as the Constitution found them, under the direction and discipline of the church or state authorities acknowledged by the several religious societies.

The aboriginal inhabitants of these countries I have regarded with the commiseration their history inspires.

...But the endeavors to enlighten them on the fate which awaits their present course of life, to induce them to exercise their reason, follow its dictates, and change their pursuits with the change of circumstances have powerful obstacles to encounter; they are combated by the habits of their bodies, prejudices of their minds, ignorance, pride, and the influence of interested and crafty individuals among them who feel themselves something in the present order of things and fear to become nothing in any other. These persons inculcate a sanctimonious reverence for the customs of their ancestors; that whatsoever they did must be done through all time, that reason is a false guide, and to advance under its counsel in their physical, moral, or political condition is perilous innovation; that their duty is to remain as their Creator made them, ignorance being safety and knowledge full of danger; in short, my friends among them also is seen the action and counteraction of good sense and of bigotry.

...I shall need, therefore, all the indulgence which I have heretofore experienced from my constituents; the want of it will certainly not lessen with increasing years. I shall need, too, the favor of that Being in whose hands we are, who led our fathers, as Israel of Old, from their native land and planted them in a country flowing with all the necessaries and comforts of life; who has covered our infancy with His providence and our riper years with His wisdom and power, and to whose goodness I ask you to join in supplications with me that He will so enlighten the minds of your servants, guide their councils, and prosper their measures that whatsoever they do shall result in your good, and shall secure to you the peace, friendship, and approbation of all nations.

JAMES MADISON
(Republican) Fourth President

b. March 16, 1751, at Port Conway, Virginia. One of 12 children.
d. June 28, 1836, at his estate Montpelier, Orange Co., Va.
m. September 15, 1794 to Dorothea "Dolly" Payne Todd, a Quaker and widow. No children together.
President from: March 4, 1809 to March 4, 1817.
1st election: won with 122 of 176 electoral votes.
2nd election: won with 128 of 219.
Father: James Madison, a planter.
Prep School: He obtained his early education from home-schooling by his parents and tutors, and later from a private school.
College: The University of New Jersey, a Presbyterian college, now known as Princeton. He and his parents chose to have him study at the University of New Jersey under the Reverend Dr. Witherspoon because they feared the "liberal" tendencies of the College of William and Mary.
Profession: Lawyer; farmer; statesman; member of Continental Congress; leader of Constitutional Convention; served in 1st Congress; founded Republican Party; Secretary of State.
Military Service: None.
Denomination: Episcopalian.
Church Service: He desired to have a career in ministry and stayed on at the University of New Jersey for a year of postgraduate study in theology.
First Inaugural: on Saturday, March 4, 1809.
Sworn in by: Chief Justice John Marshall at "The Hall of the House of Representatives" now Statuary Hall.
Second Inaugural: Thursday, March 4, 1813.
Sworn in by: Chief Justice John Marshall at the Hall of the House of Representatives.
The United States was at war with Great Britain.

JAMES MADISON
FIRST INAUGURAL ADDRESS
SATURDAY, MARCH 4, 1809

On the evening of Madison's Inauguration Day, Washington, D.C. had its first Inaugural Ball, which was held at Long's Hotel. It was also the beginning of Dolly Madison's reign as Washington's "queen of diplomacy". She had been expelled from the Friends for marrying Madison, a non-Quaker, but perhaps that gentle Quaker upbringing helped her to manage the type of graciousness she displayed at that first Inaugural Ball when she was able to have the ministers of the warring nations of France and England seated with just one person between them -- herself.

...[T]he source to which I look or the aids which alone can supply my deficiences is in the well-tried intelligence and virtue of my fellow-citizens, and in the counsels of those representing them in the other departments associated in the care of the national interests. In these my confidence will under every difficulty be best placed, next to that which we have all been encouraged to feel in the guardianship and guidance of that Almighty Being whose power regulates the destiny of nations, whose blessings have been so conspicuously dispensed to this rising Republic, and to whom we are bound to address our devout gratitude for the past, as well as our fervent supplications and best hopes for the future.

JAMES MADISON
SECOND INAUGURAL ADDRESS
THURSDAY, MARCH 4, 1813

The United States was at war with Great Britain at the time of James Madison's second inauguration. In little more than a year, however, both the Capitol and Executive Mansion would be burned by an invading British garrison, and the city thrown into a panic. At that time, the First Lady, Dolly Madison, cut the protrait of George Washington from its frame and wrapped it under her dress before she fled into Virginia.

...The impressions on me are strengthened by such an evidence that my faithful endeavors to discharge my arduous duties have been favorably estimated, and by a consideration of the momentous period at which the trust has been renewed. From the weight and magnitude now belonging to it I should be compelled to shrink if I had less reliance on the support of an enlightened and generous people, and felt less deeply a conviction that the war with a powerful nation, which forms so prominent a feature in our situation, is stamped with that justice which invites the smiles of Heaven on the means of conducting it to a successful termination.

JAMES MONROE
(Republican) Fifth President

b. April 28, 1758, at Monroe's Creek, in Westmoreland County, Va.

d. July 4, 1831 in New York City, of "old age at 73". He was the third president to die on the anniversary of Independence.

m. February 16, 1786 to Elizabeth "Eliza" Kortwright. Two daughters.

President from: March 4, 1817 to March 4, 1825.

1st Election won with 183 of 221 electoral votes.

2nd Election won with 231 of 232 (John Quincy Adams took 1).

Father: Spence Monroe, a planter.

Prep School: At a private school.

College: Studied at William and Mary but left before graduation to fight in the Revolutionary War. Later read the law for three years under Thomas Jefferson.

Profession: Soldier; Lawyer; State legislator; Senator; twice Governor of Virginia.; Minister to France and England; Secretary of State; Secretary of War; Regent, University of Virginia.

Military Service: Fought in Revolutionary War. Wounded in action at Trenton and carried the Hessian bullet in his shoulder for the rest of his life. Enlisted as a Lt. in the Continental Army under Washington. He ended the war as a Lt. Col., and he was the only soldier of the Revolution besides Washington to become President.

Denomination: Episcopalian.

First inaugural: March 4, 1817.

Sworn in by: Chief Justice John Marshall in the first outdoor inaugural. Ceremony was held on a platform adjacent to the temporary "Bride Capitol" on the grounds of the current Supreme Court Building.

Second Inaugural: March 5, 1821. This was the first time March 4th fell on a Sunday. Out of respect for the Lord's Day, upon Justice Marshall's advice Monroe waited until the following Monday to be sworn in.

He was sworn in by Justice Marshall in the Hall of the House of Representatives which had recently been rebuilt from the burning by the British invasion in 1813.

JAMES MONROE
FIRST INAUGURAL ADDRESS
TUESDAY, MARCH 4, 1817

The Capitol was under reconstruction after the fire. Speaker of the House of Representatives Henry Clay declined the use of the hall and suggested that the proceedings be held outside. The President's speech to the crowd from a platform adjacent to the brick building was the first outdoor inaugural address.

From the commencement of our Revolution to the present day almost forty years have elapsed, and from the establishment of this Constitution twenty-eight. Through this whole term the Government has been what may emphatically be called self-government. And what has been the effect? To whatever object we turn our attention, whether it relates to our foreign or domestic concerns, we find abundant cause to felicitate ourselves in the excellence of our institutions. During a period fraught with difficulties and marked by very extraordinary events the United States have been happy and the nation prosperous.

...And if we look to the condition of individuals what a proud spectacle does it exhibit!...Who has been deprived of any right of person or property? Who restrained from offering his vows in the mode which he prefers to the Divine Author of his being?...

Such, then, being the highly favored condition of our county, it is the interest of every citizen to maintain it. What are the dangers which menace us? If any exist they ought to be ascertained and guarded against...

Had the people of the United States been educated in different principles, had they been less intelligent, less independent, or less virtuous, can it be believed that we should have maintained the same steady and consistent career or been blessed with the same success? While, then, the constituent body retains its present sound and healthful state everything will be safe. They will choose competent and faithful representatives for every department. It is only when the people become ignorant and corrupt, when they degenerate into a populace, that they are incapable of exercising the sovereignty...The people themselves become the willing instruments of their own debasement and ruin...

Never did a government commence under auspices so favorable, nor ever was success so complete. If we look to the history of other nations, ancient or modern, we find no example of a growth so rapid, so gigantic, of a people so prosperous and happy. In contemplating what we have still to perform, the heart of every citizen must expand with joy when he reflects how near our Government has approached to perfection; that in respect to it we have no essential improvement to make; that the great object is to preserve it in the essential principles and features which characterize it, and that is to be done by preserving the virtue and enlightening the minds of the people; and as a security against foreign dangers to adopt such arrangements as are indispensable to the support of our independence, our rights and liberties. If we persevere in the career in which we have advanced so far and in the path already traced, we can not fail, under the favor of a gracious Providence, to attain the high destiny which seems to await us.

...Relying on the aid to be derived from the other departments of the Government, I enter on the trust to which I have been called by the suffrages of my fellow-citizens with my fervent prayers to the Almighty that He will be graciously pleased to continue to us that protection which He has already so conspicuously displayed in our favor.

JAMES MONROE
SECOND INAUGURAL ADDRESS
MONDAY, MARCH 5, 1821

In 1821, March 4 fell on a Sunday for the first time that presidential inaugurations had been observed. Although his previous term had expired on Saturday, the President waited until the following Monday, upon the advice of Chief Justice Marshall.

...In surmounting, in favor of my humble pretensions, the difficulties which so often produce division in like occurrences, it is obvious that other powerful causes, indicating the great strength and stability of our Union, have essentially contributed to draw you together. That these powerful causes exist, and that they are permanent, is my fixed opinion; that they may produce a like accord in all questions touching, however remotely, the liberty, prosperity, and happiness of our country will always be the object of my most fervent prayers to the Supreme Author of all Good.

...[I] derive great satisfaction from a knowledge that I shall be assisted in the several Departments by the very enlightened and upright citizens from whom I have received so much aid in the preceding term. With full confidence in the continuance of that candor and generous indulgence from my fellow-citizens at large which I have heretofore experienced, and with a firm reliance on the protection of Almighty God, I shall forthwith commence the duties of the high trust to which you have called me.

JOHN QUINCY ADAMS
(Republican) Sixth President

b. July 17, 1767, at Quincy, Massachusetts.

d. 80 years old, February 23, 1848, of a stroke at the Capitol while serving in Congress.

m. July 26, 1797, to Louisa Catherine Johnson, an American citizen who was born and raised in England. Three sons, one daughter.

President from: March 4, 1825 to March 4, 1829.

(Both he and his father, John Adams, were single term Presidents.)

Father: John Adams, Statesmen, 2nd President of U.S.

Prep School: Private schools in Paris, London, Amsterdam and he was enrolled for a time at the University of Leyden.

College: Completed Harvard in two years, then read for the law.

Profession: Lawyer; professor of rhetoric; Representative in Massachusetts legislature; Minister to Holland under Washington, to Prussia under his father, Russia under Madison, to England under Monroe; Secretary of State; State Senator; U.S. Senator, one term; U.S. House of Representatives, nine terms.

Military Service: None.

Denomination: Unitarian, but his definition is quite different than ours today. He wrote: "I have at all times been a sincere believer in the existence of a Supreme Creator of the world, of an immortal principle within myself, responsible to that Creator, for my conduct upon Earth, and of the divine mission of the Crucified Savior, proclaiming immortal life. . ." As President, he attended Unitarian services on Sunday morning and Presbyterian services in the afternoon. He began each morning by reading several chapters of the Bible.

Inaugural: March 4, 1825.

Sworn in by: Chief Justice John Marshall, Outside the Hall of the House of Representatives.

Noteworthy: The Presidential Campaign had 4 contestants, none of whom took a majority. John Q. Adams (Rep.) took 84 votes to Andrew Jackson (Dem.) 99. Though Jackson had more, it was still not a majority, thus pushing it into the House of Representatives. Thirteen states voted for Adams while 7 voted for Jackson and 4 for W. H. Crawford.

JOHN QUINCY ADAMS
INAUGURAL ADDRESS
FRIDAY, MARCH 4, 1825

*John Quincy Adams was chosen by the House of Representatives
when the electoral college could not determine a clear winner of the 1824
election. The outcome was assured when Henry Clay, one of the fron-
trunners, threw his support to Mr. Adams so that Andrew Jackson's candidacy would fail. General Jackson had obtained more popular votes in
the election but lost the electoral votes.*

...I appear, my fellow-citizens, in your presence and in that of
Heaven to bind myself by the solemnities of religious obligation to the
faithful performance of the duties allotted to me in the station to which I
have been called.

...The forest has fallen by the ax of our woodsmen; the soil has
been made to teem by the tillage of our farmers; our commerce has
whitened every ocean. The dominion of man over physical nature has
been extended by the invention of our artists. Liberty and law have
marched hand in hand. All the purposes of human association have been
accomplished as effectively as under any other government on the globe,
and at a cost little exceeding in a whole generation the expenditure of
other nations in a single year.

Such is the unexaggerated picture of our condition under a
Constitution founded upon the republican principle of equal rights. To
admit that this picture has its shades is but to say that it is still the condition of men upon earth. From evil - physical, moral, and political - it is
not our claim to be exempt. We have suffered sometimes by the visitation
of Heaven through disease; often by the wrongs and injustice of other
nations, even to the extremities of war; and, lastly, by dissensions among
ourselves - dissensions perhaps inseparable from the enjoyment of freedom, but which have more than once appeared to threaten the dissolution
of the Union, and with it the overthrow of all the enjoyments of our present lot and all our earthly hopes of the future.

It is a source of gratification and of encouragement to me to
observe that the great result of this experiment upon the theory of human
rights has at the close of that generation by which it was formed been
crowned with success equal to the most sanguine expectations of its

founders. Union, justice, tranquillity, the common defense, the general welfare, and the blessings of liberty - all have been promoted by the Government under which we have lived.

Fellow-citizens, you are acquainted with the peculiar circumstances of the recent election, which have resulted in affording me the opportunity of addressing you at this time...[L]ess possessed of your confidence in advance than any of my predecessors, I am deeply conscious of the prospect that I shall stand more and oftener in need of your indulgence...[T]o the guidance of the legislative councils, to the assistance of the executive and subordinate departments, to the friendly cooperation of the respective State governments, to the candid and liberal support of the people so far as it may be deserved by honest industry and zeal , I shall look for whatever success may attend my public service; and knowing that whatever success may attend my public service; and knowing that "except the Lord keep the city the watchman waketh but in vain," with fervent supplications for His favor, to His overruling providence I commit with humble but fearless confidence my own fate and the future destinies of my country.

ANDREW JACKSON
(Democrat) Seventh President

b. March 15, 1767, in the Waxhaw settlement at the North-South Carolina border. Both states say he was born on their side of the border.
d. June 8, 1845, of tuberculosis at his home at the Hermitage, near Nashville, Tennessee.
m. 1791 to Rachel (Donelson) Robards. No children together. They adopted one of a pair of twins born to Rachel's brother and named him Andrew Jackson, Jr.; they took in another relative, Andrew Jackson Donelson, and also treated him as a son.
President from: March 4, 1829 to March 4, 1837.
Father: Andrew Jackson, an Immigrant Irish linen weaver who died two weeks before Andrew's birth.
Prep School: Home schooled; self-taught, but also tutored by Dr. Wm. Humphries and the Rev. James White until age 13.
College: Self taught, read for the law.
Profession: Lawyer; Congressman; Governor; Supreme Court Judge of Tenn.; First Territorial Governor of Florida; Senator.
Military Service: Enlisted at 13 years old in the militia in the Revolutionary War, was wounded and captured by the British; both his brothers died in the war. Also fought in the Indian Wars and Battle of New Orleans against the British.
Denomination: Presbyterian.
First election: Won with 178 of 261 electoral votes. Inaugurated at the East Portico of the Capitol.
Sworn in by: Chief Justice John Marshall.
The populist President Jackson was followed home by so many well-wishers that many of the White House furnishings were ruined and Jackson had to escape out of a back window to avoid the cheerful mob.
Second election: Won with 219 of 288 electoral votes. Inaugurated inside the House of Representatives.
Sworn in by: Chief Justice John Marshall--the ninth and last time he administered the presidential oath of office, having administered all oaths except for Washington's and John Adams'.

ANDREW JACKSON
FIRST INAUGURAL ADDRESS
WEDNESDAY, MARCH 4, 1829

The election of Andrew Jackson was heralded as a new page in the history of the Republic. The first military leader elected President since George Washington, he was much admired by the electorate, who came to Washington to celebrate "Old Hickory's" inauguration. After the proceedings at the Capitol, a large group of citizens walked with the new President along Pennsylvania Avenue to the White House, and many of them visited the executive mansion that day and evening. Such large numbers of people arrived that many of the furnishings were ruined. President Jackson left the building by a window to avoid the crush of people.

Considering standing armies as dangerous to free governments in time of peace, I shall not seek to enlarge our present establishment, nor disregard that salutary lesson of political experience which teaches that the military should be held subordinate to the civil power...But the bulwark of our defense is the national militia, which in the present state of our intelligence and population must render us invincible. As long as our Government is administered for the good of the people, and is regulated by their will; as long as it secures to us the rights of person and of property, liberty of conscience and of the press, it will be worth defending; and so long as it is worth defending a patriotic militia will cover it with an impenetrable aegis. Partial injuries and occasional mortifications we may be subjected to, but a million of armed freemen, possessed of the means of war, can never be conquered by a foreign foe. To any just system, therefore, calculated to strengthen this natural safeguard of the country I shall cheerfully lend all the aid in my power...

...[D]iffidence induces me to hope for instruction and aid from the coordinate branches of the Government, and for the indulgence and support of my fellow-citizens generally. And a firm reliance on the goodness of that Power whose providence mercifully protected our national infancy, and has since upheld our liberties in various vicissitudes, encourages me to offer up my ardent supplications that He will continue to make our beloved country the object of His divine care and gracious benediction.

ANDREW JACKSON
SECOND INAUGURAL ADDRESS
MONDAY, MARCH 7, 1833

Cold weather and the President's poor health caused the second inauguration to be much quieter than the first.

...[I]t is my fervent prayer to the Almighty Being before whom I now stand, and who has kept us in His hands from the infancy of our Republic to the present day, that He will so overrule all my intentions and actions and inspire the hearts of my fellow-citizens that we may be preserved from dangers of all kinds and continue forever a united and happy people.

MARTIN VAN BUREN
(Democrat) Eighth President

b. December 5, 1782, at Kinderhook, New York, the first President to be born after the Revolution, thus the first President to be born an American citizen rather than a British subject.

d. July 24, 1862, of asthma at Lindenwald, New York

m. 1807, to Hannah Hoes, a distant cousin. Four sons.

President from: March 4, 1837 to March 4, 1841.

Won with 170 of 294 electoral votes.

Father: Abraham Van Buren, farmer and tavern keeper.

Prep School: Village schools in Kinderhook.

College: Read the law in New York City, after beginning his study of law at age 14 in Kinderhook.

Profession: Lawyer; state legislator; State Attorney General; U.S. Senator; Governor; Secretary of State; Vice President.

Military Service: None.

Denomination: Dutch Reformed Church.

Sworn in by: Chief Justice Roger Taney, at the East Portico of the Capitol.

Noteworthy: Van Buren's Vice President, Richard M. Johnson, was the only Vice President to be selected by the Senate when the electoral college could not choose.

MARTIN VAN BUREN
INAUGURAL ADDRESS
SATURDAY, MARCH 4, 1837

The ailing President Jackson and his Vice President Van Buren rode together to Van Buren's Inaugural at the Capitol in a carriage made of timbers from the U.S.S. Constitution. For the first and only time, the election for Vice President had been decided by the Senate, as provided by the constitution, when the electoral college could not select a winner.

...[I] should not dare to enter upon my path of duty did I not look for the generous aid of those who will be associated with me in the various and coordinate branches of the Government; did I not repose with unwavering reliance on the patriotism, the intelligence, and the kindness of a people who never yet deserted a public servant honestly laboring their cause; and, above all, did I not permit myself humbly to hope for the sustaining support of an ever-watchful and beneficent Providence...

...[I] only look to the gracious protection of the Divine Being whose strengthening support I humbly solicit, and whom I fervently pray to look down upon us all. May it be among the dispensations of His providence to bless our beloved country with honors and with length of days. May her ways be ways of pleasantness and all her paths be peace!

WILLIAM HENRY HARRISON
(Whig) Ninth President

b. February 9, 1773 at Berkeley, Charles City Co., Virginia.

d. April 4, 1841 of pneumonia, resulting from giving the longest inaugural speech in history during a snowstorm.

m. 1795 to Anna Symmes. Six sons, four daughters.

President from: March 4, 1841 to April 4, 1841.

Won with 234 of 294 electoral votes.

Father: Planter Benjamin Harrison, a signer of the Declaration (William Henry Harison's son, John Scott Harrison, was in Congress when he was President, and his Grandson, Benjamin Harrison became the 23rd President).

Prep School: Home-schooled.

College: Hampden-Sidney College, Prince Edward County, Va.

Studied medicine, but quit to go fight the Indians.

Profession: Soldier; Secretary of the Northwest Territory; Northwest Territory delegate to Congress; Governor of Indiana Territory; U.S. Representative from Ohio; State Senator; U.S. Senator; Minister to Colombia; Superintendent of Indian Affairs; minor local and county offices; farmer.

Military Service: Fought Indians in the West against Tecumseh; fought England in War of 1812, commanding the forces in the Northwest, invading Canada.

Denomination: Episcopalian; he read the Bible daily and attended church regularly.

Sworn in by: Chief Justice Roger Taney, at the East Portico of the Capitol (his inaugural speech was the longest: 8,495 words. In contrast, Washington's second inaugural speech was the shortest: 135 words).

Noteworthy: Harrison was the first President to die in office, and he had the shortest term of any president.

WILLIAM HENRY HARRISON
INAUGURAL ADDRESS
THURSDAY, MARCH 4, 1841

President Harrison has the dual distinction among all the Presidents of giving the longest inaugural speech and of serving the shortest term of office. He delivered an hour-and-forty-five-minute speech (8,495 words) in a snowstorm. The 68-year-old President stood outside for the entire proceeding. One month later he died of pneumonia.

However strong may be my present purpose to realize the expectations of a magnanimous and confiding people, I too well understand the dangerous temptations to which I shall be exposed from the magnitude of the power which it has been the pleasure of the people to commit to my hands not to place my chief confidence upon the aid of that Almighty Power which has hitherto protected me and enabled me to bring to favorable issues other important but still greatly inferior trusts heretofore confided to me by my country...

The majority of our citizens... possess a sovereignty with an amount of power precisely equal to that which has been granted to them by the parties to the national compact, and nothing beyond. We admit of no government by divine right, believing that so far as power is concerned the Beneficent Creator has made no distinction amongst men; that all are upon an equality, and that the only legitimate right to govern is an express grant of power from the governed...

...The power of our sovereignty... can interfere with no one's faith, prescribe forms of worship for no one's observance, inflict no punishment but after well-ascertained guilt, the result of investigation under rules prescribed by the Constitution itself. These precious privileges, and those scarcely less important of giving experession to his thoughts and opinions, either by writing or speaking, unrestrained but by the liability for injury to others, and that of a full participation in all the advantages which flow from the Government, the acknowledged property of all, the American citizen derives from no charter granted by his fellow-man. He claims them because he is himself a man, fashioned by the same Almighty hand as the rest of his species and entitled to a full share of the blessings with which He has endowed them...

The great dread of the patriots who opposed adoption of our current Government seems to have been that the reserved powers of the States would be absorbed by those of the Federal Government and a consolidated power established, leaving to the States the shadow only of that independent action for which they had so zealously contended and on the preservation of which they relied as the last hope of liberty...

The tendencies of all such governments in their decline is to monarchy, and the antagonist principle to liberty there is the spirit of faction - a spirit which assumes the character and in times of great excitement imposes itself upon the people as the genuine spirit of freedom, and, like the false christs whose coming was foretold by the Savior, seeks to, and were it possible would, impose upon the true and most faithful disciples of liberty...

...I deem the present occasion sufficiently important and solemn to justify me in expressing to my fellow-citizens a profound reverence for the Christian religion and a thorough conviction that sound morals, religious liberty, and a just sense of religious responsibility are essentially connected with all true and lasting happiness; and to that good Being who has blessed us by the gifts of civil and religious freedom, who watched over and prospered the labors of our fathers and has hitherto preserved to us institutions far exceeding in excellence those of any other people, let us unite in fervently commending every interest of our beloved country in all future time.

JOHN TYLER
(Democrat/Whig) Tenth President

b. March 29, 1790, at Greenway, Charles City Co., Virginia.

d. January 17, 1862 "of a bilious attack".

m. 1813, to Letitia Christian, three sons, four daughters. She died in 1842.

m. 1844, to Julia Gardiner, Five sons, two daughters.

President from: April 4, 1841 to March 4, 1845.

Was Harrison's Vice President and filled the Presidency upon Harrison's death. During Tyler's term, there was no Vice President.

Father: Judge John Tyler.

Prep School: A grammar school associated with the College of William and Mary.

College: William and Mary, and read the law with his father and Edmund Randolph.

Profession: Lawyer; State legislator; twice Governor of Virginia; chancellor of William and Mary; U.S. Representative; U.S. Senator; Vice President; sat in the provisional Confederate Congress, was elected to the Confederate House, but died before taking his seat.

Military Service: Militia captain in the War of 1812, but never saw action.

Denomination: Episcopalian.

No inaugural speech given.

Sworn in by: U.S. Circuit Court Judge William Cranch.

Noteworthy: Both Tyler and the President he succeeded were elected not only from the same state, but also from the same county.

Given the oath of office at Mr. Tyler's residence at The Indian Queen Hotel on April 6, 1841.

JAMES KNOX POLK
(Democrat) Eleventh President

b. November 2, 1795, Mecklenburg County, North Carolina.

d. June 15, 1849, died 3 months after leaving office of chronic diarrhea, at Nashville.

m. 1824 to Sarah Childress, no children.

President from: March 4, 1845 to March 4, 1849.

Won with 170 of 275 electoral votes.

Father: Samuel Polk, a farmer,surveyor.

Prep School: Primarily home-schooled, but he attended a Presbyterian academy for one year prior to entering the state university.

College: University of North Carolina, read the law in Nashville.

Profession: Lawyer; state legislator; seven-term Congressman; Governor of Tennessee.

Military Service: None.

Denomination: Presbyterian and Methodist. He was raised a Presbyterian and regularly attended Presbyterian services throughout his life. However, at a camp revival meeting in 1833 he was profoundly moved by the preaching of Methodist Reverend John B. McFerrin. He continued to worship with his wife at their Presbyterian church, but on his deathbed he asked for Rev. McFerrin who then baptized Polk as a Methodist.

Inaugurated at: The East Portico of the Capitol.

Sworn in by: Chief Justice Roger Taney.

Noteworthy: This was the first inaugural to be reported by modern communications: a report of the events was transmitted to Baltimore by Samuel Morse on the telegrapher he had invented a year before.

JAMES KNOX POLK
INAUGURAL ADDRESS
TUESDAY, MARCH 4, 1845

President Polk and his wife Sarah (who had been educated at the Moravian Female Academy) carried their strong faith into the White House with them even though it was not always socially convenient. Although President Polk had shouted his Inaugural Address through a cold and driving rain "to a large assemblage of umbrellas", as John Quincy Adams described it, the evening's Inauguration Ball was dry -- no liquor, no dancing, no card playing. Their term in office was marked by their constant companionship, their hard work, and their willingness to bring to church with them anyone who happened to be present at the White House on Sunday morning.

...In assuming responsibilities so vast I fervently invoke the aid of that Almighty Ruler of the Universe in whose hands are the destinies of nations and of men to guard this Heaven-favored land against the mischiefs which without His guidance might arise from an unwise public policy. With a firm reliance upon the wisdom of Omnipotence to sustain and direct me in the path of duty which I am appointed to pursue, I stand in the presence of this assembled multitude of my countrymen to take upon myself the solemn obligation "to the best of my ability to preserve, protect, and defend the Constitution of the United States."

...To the Government of the United States has been intrusted the exclusive management of our foreign affairs. Beyond that it wields a few general enumerated powers. It does not force reform on the States. It leaves individuals, over whom it casts its protecting influence, entirely free to improve their own conditon by the legitimate exercise of all their mental and physical powers. It is a common protector of each and all the States; of every man who lives upon our soil, whether of native or foreign birth; of every religious sect, in their worship of the Almighty according to the dictates of their own conscience; of every shade of opinion, and the most free inquiry; of every art, trade, and occupation consistent with the laws of the States. And we rejoice in the general happiness, prosperity, and advancement of our county, which have been the offspring of freedom, and not of power.

This most admirable and wisest system of well-regulated self-government... will, I fervently hope and believe, endure for ages to come and dispense the blessings of civil and religious liberty to distant generations.

...Confidently relying upon the aid and assistance of the coordinate departments of the Government in conducting our public affairs, I enter upon the discharge of the high duties which have been assigned me by the people, again humbly supplicating that Divine Being who has watched over and protected our beloved country from its infancy to the present hour to continue His gracious benedictions upon us, that we may continue to be a prosperous and happy people.

ZACHARY TAYLOR
(Whig) Twelfth President

b. November 24, 1784, Montebello, Orange County, Virginia.

d. July 9, 1850 of "a bilious fever" at the White House.

m. To Margaret Smith, one son, five daughters.

President from: March 5, 1849 (March 4th, again fell on a Sunday and Taylor waited until Monday to become President). to July 9, 1850.

Father: Col. Richard Taylor, a Revolutionary War Soldier and Collector of the Port, Louisville, Kentucky.

Prep School: Primarily home-schooled.

College: None.

Profession: Soldier. Joined the Kentucky militia in his late teens, fought in the Northwest, in Florida, in the Blackhawk War, commanded the Southwest Department, fought in the Mexican-American War where he overthrew Santa Ana at Buena Vista. Farmer. Purchased a plantation while stationed at Louisiana, was a slave-owner.

Military Service: See Profession.

Denomination: Episcopalian.

Inaugurated at: The East Portico of the Capitol.

Sworn in by: Chief Justice Roger Taney.

Noteworthy: He had never even voted in a national election until his own Presidency.

ZACHARY TAYLOR
INAUGURAL ADDRESS
MONDAY, MARCH 5, 1849

For the second time in the history of the Republic, March 4 fell on a Sunday. The inaugural ceremony was postponed until the following Monday. Zachary Taylor was not a politician, in fact, he never had voted in a national election until his own contest for the Presidency.

...I congratulate you, my fellow-citizens, upon the high state of prosperity to which the goodness of Divine Providence has conducted our common country. Let us invoke a continuance of the same protecting care which has led us from small beginnings to the eminence we this day occupy, and let us seek to deserve that continuance by prudence and moderation in our councils, by well-directed attempts to assuage the bitterness which too often marks unavoidable differences of opinion, by the promulgation and practice of just and liberal principles, and by an enlarged patriotism, which shall acknowledge no limits but those of our own widespread Republic.

MILLARD FILLMORE
(Whig) Thirteenth President

b. January 7, 1800, Cayuga County, New York.

d. March 8, 1874, at Buffalo, New York.

m. 1826 to Abigail Powers (the daughter of a minister), one son, one daughter.

Abigail died 1853 after catching cold at his successor's inauguration.

m. 1858 to Caroline (Carmichael) McIntosh, widow of wealthy Albany merchant. No children.

Father: Nathaniel Fillmore, a log cabin settler.

Prep School: The story is told that the only two books he had seen before he was 15 were the Bible and a hymnbook. Home-schooled. village schools, apprenticed to a tailor, tutored by his wife who was a school teacher.

College: Read for the law and passed the N.Y. bar in 1832.

Profession: Tailor; Teacher; Lawyer; State Legislator; Congressman; Comptroller of New York; Vice President.

Military Service: None.

Denomination: Unitarian.

President from: July 10, 1850 to March 4, 1853.

No inaugural speech. Oath of office taken at the Hall of the House of Representatives on July 10, 1850.

Sworn in by: U.S. Circuit Court Judge William Cranch.

Noteworthy: He had no Vice President. He was nominated for president in 1856 by the "Know-Nothing" party but was defeated by Buchanan.

FRANKLIN PIERCE
(Democrat) Fourteenth President

b. November 23, 1804, at Hillsborough, N.H., the first President born in the 19th Century.

d. October 8, 1869 of stomach trouble, at Concord, N.H.

m. 1834 to Jane Means Appleton of N.H., daughter of Reverend Appleton, a Congregational minister. Three sons who all died before adulthood.

Father: Gen. Benjamin Pierce: Farmer, Governor and officer of the revolutionary army.

Prep School: Village elementary school, then academies at Hancock and Francestown.

College: Bowdoin College; read the law at Portsmouth, N.H., Northampton Massachusetts and Amherst, New Hampshire.

Profession: Lawyer; State Legislator; U.S. Representative; U.S. Senator (youngest of his day); Federal District Attorney for New Hampshire; retired from public service and declined nominations for Senator and Governor and appointment for U.S. Attorney General.

Military Service: When the Mexican war was declared, he enlisted as a private and finished as a brig. general.

Denomination: Episcopalian; as a college student he knelt nightly with his roommate to say prayers. As President, he read each morning from Thornton's Family Prayers, attended church regularly, said grace at each meal, and would not even read mail on the Lord's Day.

President from: March 4, 1853 to March 4, 1857.

Inaugurated at: the East Portico of the Capitol.

Sworn in by: Chief Justice Roger Taney.

He is the only president to have chosen to "affirm" rather than swear for religious reasons.

Noteworthy: Shortly before his inaugural, the Pierces' last surviving child was killed in a train wreck.

FRANKLIN PIERCE
INAUGURAL ADDRESS
FRIDAY, MARCH 4, 1853

On religious grounds, former Senator and Congressman Franklin Pierce chose "to affirm" rather than "to swear" the executive oath of office. He was the only President to use the choice offered by the Constitution. He was nominated as the Democratic candidate in the national convention on the 49th ballot. Several weeks before arriving in Washington, the Pierces' only surviving child had been killed in a train accident.

...Preeminently, the power of our advocacy reposes in our example; but no example, be it remembered, can be powerful for lasting good, whatever apparent advantages may be gained, which is not based upon eternal principles of right and justice. Our fathers decided for themselves, both upon the hour to declare and the hour to strike. They were their own judges of the circumstances under which it became them to pledge to each other "their lives, their fortunes, and their sacred honor" for the acquisition of the priceless inheritance transmitted to us. The energy with which that great conflict was opened and, under the guidance of a manifest and beneficent Providence the uncomplaining endurance with which it was prosecuted to its consummation were only surpassed by the wisdom and patriotic spirit of concession which characterized all the counsels of the early fathers...

...With the Union my best and dearest earthly hopes are entwined. Without it what are we individually or collectively? What becomes of the noblest field ever opened for the advancement of our race in religion, in government, in the arts, and in all that dignifies and adorns mankind? From that radiant constellation which both illumines our own way and points out to struggling nations their course, let but a single star be lost, and, if these be not utter darkness, the luster of the whole is dimmed. Do my countrymen need any assurance that such a catastrophe is not to overtake them while I possess the power to stay it? It is with me an earnest and vital belief that as the Union has been the source, under Providence, of our prosperity to this time, so it is the surest pledge of a continuance of the blessings we have enjoyed, and which we are sacredly bound to transmit undiminished to our children.

...But let not the foundation of our hope rest upon man's wisdom.

It will not be sufficient that sectional prejudices find no place in the public deliberations. It will not be sufficient that the rash counsels of human passion are rejected. It must be felt that there is no national security but in the nation's humble, acknowledged dependence upon God and His overruling providence...

...Let it be impressed upon all hearts that, beautiful as our fabric is, no earthly power or wisdom could ever reunite its broken fragments. Standing, as I do, almost within view of the green slopes of Monticello, and, as it were, within reach of the tomb of Washington, with all the cherished memories of the past gathering around me like so many eloquent voices of exhortation from heaven, I can express no better hope for my country than that the kind Providence which smiled upon our fathers may enable their children to preserve the blessings they have inherited.

JAMES BUCHANAN
(Democrat) Fifteenth President

b. April 23, 1791, at Stony Batter near Mercersburg, Pennsylvania.

d. June 1, 1868 of rheumatic gout at age 77, at Wheatland, near Lancaster, Pa.

m. Never married.

Father: James Buchanan, a merchant and farmer.

Prep School: Local elementary school and an academy.

College: Dickinson College, read the law at Lancaster, Pennsylvania.

Profession: Lawyer; Soldier; State Legislator; Senator; Congressman; Secretary of State; Ambassador to Russia; Minister to Great Britain.

Military Service: Volunteered in a dragoon unit in the War of 1812.

Denomination: Presbyterian. He wrote to his brother, who was a minister, "I can say sincerely for myself that I desire to be a Christian." He prayed daily, conducted personal Bible study and strictly observed the Lord's Day.

President from: March 4, 1857 to March 4, 1861.

Inaugurated at: The East Portico of the Capitol.

Sworn in by: Chief Justice Roger Taney.

Noteworthy: He is the only president to have never married. He ordered in his will that his love letters with his fianceé who died suddenly be destroyed without inspection. His niece, Harriet Lane, acted as his White House hostess and First Lady.

JAMES BUCHANAN
INAUGURAL ADDRESS
WEDNESDAY, MARCH 4, 1857

Two days after his Inauguration, the Supreme Court released its Dred Scott decision, greatly complicating any hope of compromise on the slavery issue. Later that year, a financial panic erupted bankrupting 5000 companies. John Brown was stirring up guerrilla war in Kansas, which had rejected statehood unless it could have it without slavery. The Mormons in Utah killed 120 immigrants and attacked an Army supply unit. In the year of his inauguration, the States did not appear very United.

...In entering upon this great office I must humbly invoke the God of our fathers for wisdom and firmness to execute its high and responsible duties in such a manner as to restore harmony and ancient friendship among the people of the several States and to perserve our free institutions throughout many generations. Convinced that I owe my election to the inherent love for the Constitution and the Union which still animates the hearts of the American people, let me earnestly ask their powerful support in sustaining all just measures calculated to perpetuate these, the richest political blessings which Heaven has ever bestowed upon any nation...

...I feel an humble confidence that the kind Providence which inspired our fathers with wisdom to frame the most perfect form of government and union ever devised by man will not suffer it to perish until it shall have been peacefully instrumental by its example in the extension of civil and religious liberty throughout the world...

...It may be proper that on this occasion I should make some brief remarks in regard to our rights and duties as a member of the great family of nations. In our intercourse with them there are some plain principles, approved by our own experience, from which we should never depart. We ought to cultivate peace, commerce, and friendship with all nations, and this not merely as the best means of promoting our own material interests, but in a spirit of Christian benevolence toward our fellow-men, wherever their lot may be cast...

...I shall now proceed to take the oath prescribed by the Constitution, whilst humbly invoking the blessing of Divine Providence on this great people.

ABRAHAM LINCOLN
(Republican) Sixteenth President

b. February 12, 1809, Hardin (now Larue) County, Kentucky.

d. April 15, 1865 age 56, killed by assassin's bullet.

m. 1842 to Mary Todd. Four sons, only one of whom survived to adulthood.

Father: Thomas Lincoln, a pioneer settler, farmer, carpenter.

Prep School: Self taught; home-schooled; Lincoln had a combined lifetime total of one year of formal education.

College: Read for the law in New Salem, Illinois.

Profession: Farmer; ferryman; storekeeper; surveyor; lawyer; postmaster; State legislator; U.S. Congressman.

Military Service: 1832, enlisted as a private in the Blackhawk War. He said his election as captain by his men was the most satisfying election he'd had.

Denomination: As President, he attended the First Presbyterian Church and New York Avenue Presbyterian Church but referred to himself simply as "Christian".

President from: March 4, 1861 to April 15, 1865.

First Inaugural: March 4th, 1861 at East Portico of the Capitol. Lincoln was the ninth and last president sworn in by Chief Justice Roger Taney. Jefferson Davis two weeks earlier had been sworn in as President of the Confederacy. To avoid a rumored ambush, Lincoln traveled to his inauguration by a secret route. He had won the Presidency with a plurality of less than 40% of the votes over a 4 man field.

Second Inaugural: March 4th, 1865 on the East Portico, sworn in by Chief Justice Salmon Chase.

Noteworthy: Lincoln's election to a second term broke the streak of 8 consecutive one-term presidents.

ABRAHAM LINCOLN
FIRST INAUGURAL ADDRESS
MONDAY, MARCH 4, 1861

Jefferson Davis had been inaugurated as the President of the Confederacy two weeks earlier.

...Why should there not be a patient confidence in the ultimate justice of the people? Is there any better or equal hope in the world? In our present differences, is either party without faith of being in the right? If the Almighty Ruler of Nations, with His eternal truth and justice, be on your side of the North, or on yours of the South, that truth and that justice will surely prevail by the judgment of this great tribunal of the American people.

By the frame of the Government under which we live this same people have wisely given their public servants but little power for mischief, and have with equal wisdom provided for the return of that little to their own hands at very short intervals. While the people retain their virtue and vigilance no Administration by any extreme of wickedness or folly can very seriously injure the Government in the short space of four years.

My countrymen, one and all, think calmly and well upon this whole subject. Nothing valuable can be lost by taking time...Intelligence, patriotism, Christianity, and a firm reliance on Him who has never yet forsaken this favored land are still competent to adjust in the best way all our present difficulty.

In your hands, my dissatisfied fellow-countrymen, and not in mine, is the momentous issue of civil war. The Government will not assail you. You can have no conflict without being yourselves the aggressors. You have no oath registered in heaven to destroy the Government, while I shall have the most solemn one to "preserve, protect, and defend it"...

ABRAHAM LINCOLN
SECOND INAUGURAL ADDRESS
SATURDAY, MARCH 4, 1865

Thousands of spectators stood in thick mud at the Capitol grounds to hear the President. In little more than a month, the President would be assassinated.

At this second appearing to take the oath of the Presidential office there is less occasion for an extended address than there was at the first...

On the occasion corresponding to this four years ago all thoughts were anxiously directed to an impending civil war...Both parties deprecated war, but one of them would make war rather than let the nation survive, and the other would accept war rather than let it perish, and the war came.

One-eighth of the whole population were colored slaves, not distributed generally over the Union, but localized in the southern part of it. These slaves constituted a peculiar and powerful interest. All knew that this interest was somehow the cause of the war...Neither party expected for the war the magnitude or the duration which it has already attained. Neither anticipated that the cause of the conflict might cease with or even before the conflict itself should cease. Each looked for an easier triumph, and a result less fundamental and astounding. Both read the same Bible and pray to the same God, and each invokes His aid against the other. It may seem strange that any men should dare to ask a just God's assistance in wringing their bread from the sweat of other men's faces, but let us judge not, that we be not judged. The prayers of both could not be answered. That of neither has been answered fully. The Almighty has His own purposes. "Woe unto the world because of offenses; for it must needs be that offenses come, but woe to that man by whom the offense cometh." If we shall suppose that American slavery is one of those offenses which, in the providence of God, must needs come, but which, having continued through His appointed time, He now wills to remove, and that He gives to both North and South this terrible war as the woe due to those by whom the offense came, shall we discern therein any departure from those divine attributes which the believers in a living God always ascribe to Him? Fondly do we hope, fervently do we pray, that this mighty scourge of war may speedily pass away. Yet, if God wills that it continue until all the wealth piled by the bondsman's two hundred and fifty years of unrequited toil shall be sunk, and until every drop of blood drawn with the lash shall be paid by another drawn with the sword, as was said three thousand years ago, so still it must be said "the judgments of the Lord are true and righteous altogether."

With malice toward none, with charity for all, with firmness in the right as God gives us to see the right, let us strive on to finish the work we are in, to bind up the nation's wounds, to care for him who shall have borne the battle and for his widow and his orphan, to do all which may achieve and cherish a just and lasting peace among ourselves and with all nations.

ANDREW JOHNSON
(Republican) Seventeenth President

b. December 29, 1808, Raleigh, North Carolina.

d. July 31, 1875 of paralysis.

m. 1827 to Eliza McCardle, three sons, two daughters.

Father: Jacob Johnson, a sexton (a church janitor) and constable. Died while rescuing a man from drowning.

Prep School: Never attended any school, self-educated. He could not read or write until his wife, a teacher, helped him learn.

College: None, apprenticed to a tailor at 13.

Profession: Tailor, alderman, Mayor of Greenville, Tennessee; state legislator; four term Congressman; two term Governor; Vice President; U.S. Senator (after he had served as President).

Military Service: Named by Lincoln as Military Governor of Tennessee.

Denomination: Methodist.

President from: April 15, 1865 to March 4, 1869.

Oath of office taken: At his rooms at Kirkwood House, on April 15, 1865. Sworn in by Chief Justice Salmon Chase.

Noteworthy: When he tried to fire his Secretary of War, Edwin M. Stanton, his opponents claimed that in doing so he had violated a new civil servant's law. He narrowly escaped impeachment by only one vote.

No inaugural speech.

ULYSSES SIMPSON GRANT
(Republican) Eighteenth President

b. April 27, 1822, Point Pleasant Ohio, born as Hirem Ulysses Grant.

d. July 23, 1885 of cancer, age 63.

m. 1848 to Julia Dent; three sons and one daughter.

Father: Jesse R. Grant, a tanner.

Prep School: Local schools, also academies in Maysville, Ky., and Ripley, Ohio.

College: United States Military Academy at West Point, graduated 21st of 39 in his class.

Profession: Career soldier; farmer; real estate speculator; store clerk; bill collector.

Military Service: Attended West Point, served in Mexican War, forced to resign in 1854 due to problems resulting from his alcoholism. Began Civil War as a volunteer militia.

Denomination: Methodist.

President from: March 4, 1869 to March 4, 1877.

First Inaugural at: East Portico.

Sworn in by: Chief Justice Salmon Chase.

Ironically, although his speech focused on reconciliation of the Nation's factions, he refused to ride to the inauguration with Andrew Johnson.

Second Inaugural: at East Portico (sparsely attended due to the zero-degree weather).

Sworn in by: Chief Justice Salmon Chase.

ULYSSES S. GRANT
FIRST INAUGURAL ADDRESS
THURSDAY, MARCH 4, 1869

General Grant refused to ride in the carriage to the Capitol with President Johnson, who then decided not to attend the ceremony. Compare this conduct with General Grant's admonition for "patient forbearance one toward another" in the last paragraph of his speech.

...The country having just emerged from a great rebellion, many questions will come before it for settlement in the next four years which preceding Administrations have never had to deal with. In meeting these it is desirable that they should be approached calmly, without prejudice, hate, or sectional pride, remembering that the greatest good to the greatest number is the object to be attained.

This requires security of person, property, and free religious and political opinion in every part of our common country, without regard to local prejudice. All laws to secure these ends will receive my best efforts for their enforcement...

...When we compare the paying capacity of the country now, with the ten States in poverty from the effects of war, but soon to emerge, I trust, into greater prosperity than ever before, with its paying capacity twenty-five years ago, and calculate what it probably will be twenty-five years hence, who can doubt the feasibility of paying every dollar then with more ease than we now pay for useless luxuries? Why, it looks as though Providence had bestowed upon us a strong box in the precious metals locked up in the sterile mountains of the far West, and which we are now forging the key to unlock, to meet the very contingency that is now upon us.

...In conclusion I ask patient forbearance one toward another throughout the land, and a determined effort on the part of every citizen to do his share toward cementing a happy union; and I ask the prayers of the nation to Almighty God in behalf of this consummation.

ULYSSES S. GRANT
SECOND INAUGURAL ADDRESS
TUESDAY, MARCH 4, 1873

Grant had narrowly escaped defeat in his re-election bid. His opponent was newspaperman Horace Greely who died shortly after the popular election but before the electoral votes were cast. At the Inaugural Ball, for his re-election, planning was so poor that guests were compelled to leave because of the total lack of heat in the cold January night. General Grant may have been able to have things accomplished, but President Grant was not.

Under Providence I have been called a second time to act as Executive over this great nation. It has been my endeavor in the past to maintain all the laws, and, so far as lay in my power, to act for the best interests of the whole people.

...In future, while I hold my present office, the subject of acquisition of territory must have the support of the people before I will recommend any proposition looking to such acquisition. I say here, however, that I do not share in the apprehension held by many as to the danger of governments becoming weakened and destroyed by reason of their extension of territory. Commerce, education, and rapid transit of thought and matter by telegraph and steam have changed all this. Rather do I believe that our Great Maker is preparing the world, in His own good time, to become one nation, speaking one language, and when armies and navies will be no longer required...

RUTHERFORD B. HAYES
(Republican) Nineteenth President

b. October 4, 1822, at Delaware, Ohio.

d. January 17, 1893 of heart disease, age 70.

m. 1852 to Lucy Ware Webb, seven sons, one daughter.

Father: Rutherford B. Hayes, a farmer and merchant who died shortly before his son's birth.

Prep School: Private tutors and academies at Norwalk, Ohio and Middletown, Connecticut.

College: Kenyon College, Harvard Law School.

Profession: Lawyer; City Solicitor; Soldier; Congressman; three term Governor.

Military Service: Brevet Maj. General in the Civil War.

Denomination: Methodist. As President he started a practice of conducting Sunday evening group hymn sings at the White House.

President from: March 3, 1877 (March 4th was a Sunday so he took one oath on Saturday and another public one on Monday) to March 4, 1881. Inaugurated at the Red Room of the White House on March 3, the East Portico of the Capitol on March 5.

Sworn in by: Chief Justice Morrison Waite both times.

Noteworthy: The election was marred by many irregularities and accusations of fraud. This must have been particularly painful for Hayes, who once had been dubbed "The Golden Rule Incarnate," and who was introduced to a Harvard audience by Oliver Wendell Holmes as "His Honesty". Hayes had less of the popular vote than Tilden, his Democratic opponent. The House of Representatives could not decide on the 20 disputed electoral votes and created a commission of five Representatives, 5 Senators and 5 Supreme Court judges to decide the contested votes.

The composition of the Commission was 8 Republicans and 7 Democrats. Each vote contest was won for Republican Hayes by a vote of 8 to 7 and he was elected by a margin of one electoral vote.

An interesting political sidelight is that at one point during Hayes' presidency a U.S. Senator from Mississippi, a black man named Blanche K. Bruce, presided over the Senate briefly and thus was technically next in line for the Presidency.

RUTHERFORD B. HAYES
INAUGURAL ADDRESS
MONDAY, MARCH 5, 1877

The outcome of the election of 1876 was not known until the week before the inauguration itself. Democrat Samuel Tilden had won the greater number of popular votes and lacked only one electoral vote to claim a majority in the electoral college. Twenty disputed electoral votes, however, kept hopes alive for Republican Governor Hayes of Ohio. A fifteen-member Electoral Commission was appointed by the Congress to deliberate the outcome of the election. By a majority vote of 8 to 7 the Commission gave all of the disputed votes to the Republican candidate, and Mr. Hayes was elected President on March 2. Since March 4 was a Sunday, he took the oath of office in the Red Room at the White House on March 3, and again on Monday on the East Portico of the Capitol.

...[A]t the basis of all prosperity, for [the South] as well as for every other part of the country, lies the improvement of the intellectual and moral condition of the people. Universal suffrage should rest upon universal education. To this end, liberal and permanent provision should be made for the support of free schools by the State governments, and, if need be, supplemented by legitimate aid from national authority...

...For the first time in the history of the country it has been deemed best, in view of the peculiar circumstances of the case, that the objections and questions in dispute with reference to the counting of the electoral votes should be referred to the decision of a tribunal appointed for this purpose...

For the present, opinion will widely vary as to the wisdom of the several conclusions announced by that tribunal. This is to be anticipated in every instance where matters of dispute are made the subject of arbitration under the forms of law. Human judgment is never unerring, and is rarely regarded as otherwise than wrong by the unsuccessful party in the contest...

Looking for the guidance of that Divine Hand by which the destinies of nations and individuals are shaped, I call upon you Senators, Representatives, judges, fellow-citizens, here and everywhere, to unite with me in an earnest effort to secure to our country the blessings, not only of material prosperity, but of justice, peace, and union -- a union depending not upon the constraint of force, but upon the loving devotion of a free people; "and that all things may be so ordered and settled upon the best and surest foundations that peace and happiness, truth and justice, religion and piety, may be established among us for all generations."

JAMES ABRAM GARFIELD
(Republican) Twentieth President

b. November 19, 1831 at Orange, Cuyahoga County, Ohio, the last president to be born in a log cabin.

d. September 19, 1881 age 50, 80 days after the wounds from an assassin's bullet

m. 1858, to Lecretia Rudolph. Four sons, one daughter.

Father: Abram Garfield, "a pioneer of the west", who died when he was 2 years old.

Prep School: Geauga Seminary, a Free Will Baptist school, in Hiram, Ohio.

College: Western Reserve Electric Institute, Williams College, a Disciples of Christ school.

Profession: Canal bargemen; farmer; carpenter; teacher; college president; state senator; lawyer; soldier; Congressman.

Military Service: Enlisted when the Civil War erupted, rose to General.

Denomination: Disciples of Christ Church.

Church Service: During his student days and later he served as a minister, held revivals, baptized new believers.

President from: March 4, 1881 to September 19, 1881.

Inaugurated at: East Portico of the Capitol.

Sworn in by: Chief Justice Morrison Waite.

Noteworthy: Though Garfield's denomination had a strongly pacifist tradition, the Garfields believed he should enlist to fight slavery. He wrote a friend, "[We] believe the sin of slavery is one of which it may be said that without the shedding of blood there is no remission."

Garfield came to national attention when, upon hearing that Lincoln had been assasinated, he said, "Clouds and darkness are around Him; His pavilion is dark waters and thick clouds; justice and judgment are the habitation of His throne; mercy and truth shall go before His face! Fellow citizens, God reigns and the Government at Washington still lives!"

JAMES A. GARFIELD
INAUGURAL ADDRESS
FRIDAY, MARCH 4, 1881

Snow on the ground discouraged many spectators from attending the ceremony at the Capitol. Congressman Garfield had been nominated on his party's 36th ballot at the convention; and he had won the popular vote by a slim margin. John Philip Sousa led the Marine Corps band.

...It is now three days more than a hundred years since the adoption of the first written constitution of the United States - the Articles of Confederation and Perpetual Union...

...We can not overestimate the fervent love of liberty, the intelligent courage, and the sum of common sense with which our fathers made the great experiment of self-government...

...The will of the nation, speaking with the voice of battle and through the amended Constitution, has fulfilled the great promise of 1776 by proclaiming "liberty throughout the land to all the inhabitants thereof."

The elevation of the negro race from slavery to the full rights of citizenship is the most important political change we have known since the adoption of the constitution of 1787...

...The emanicipated race has already made remarkable progress. With unquestioning devotion to the Union, with a patience and gentleness not born of fear, they have "followed the light as God gave them to see the light"...

...In this beneficent work sections and races should be forgotten and partisanship should be unknown. Let our people find a new meaning in the divine oracle which declares that "a little child shall lead them," for our own little children will soon control the destinies of the Republic.

My countrymen, we do not now differ in our judgment concerning the controversies of past generations, and fifty years hence our children will not be divided in their opinions concerning our controversies. They will surely bless their fathers and their fathers' God that the Union was preserved, that slavery was overthrown, and that both races were made equal before the law.

...The Constitution guarantees absolute religious freedom. Congress is prohibited from making any law respecting an establishment of religion or prohibiting the free exercise thereof. The Territories of the United States are subject to the direct legislative authority of Congress, and hence the General Government is responsible for any violation of the constitution in any of them. It is therefore a reproach to the Government that in the most populous of the Territories the constitutional guaranty is not enjoyed by the people and the authority of congress is set at naught. The Mormon Church not only offends the moral sense of manhood by sanctioning polygamy, but prevents the administration of justice through ordinary instrumentalities of law.

In my judgment it is the duty of congress, while respecting to the uttermost the conscientious convictions and religious scruples of every citizen, to prohibit within its jurisdiction all criminal practices, especially of that class which destroy the family relations and endanger social order. Nor can any ecclesiastical organization be safely permitted to usurp in the smallest degree the functions and powers of the National Government.

...And now, fellow-citizens, I am about to assume the great trust which you have committed to my hands...

...I shall greatly rely upon the wisdom and patriotism of Congress and of those who may share with me the responsibilities and duties of administration, and, above all, upon our efforts to promote the welfare of this great people and their Government I reverently invoke the support and blessings of Almighty God.

CHESTER ALAN ARTHUR
(Republican) Twenty-First President

b. October 5, 1830 at Fairfield, Vermont.
d. November 18, 1886 of Bright's disease, age 56.
m. 1859, Ellen Lewis Herndon, two sons, one daughter.
Father: Rev. William Arthur, a Baptist preacher.
College: Union College.
Profession: Teacher; lawyer; Inspector General; Quartermaster General of New York; Collector of Port of New York.
Military Service: None.
Denomination: Episcopalian.
President: From September 20, 1881 to March 4, 1885.
Sworn in by: New York Supreme Court Judge John R. Brady on September 20, 1881: Oath of office taken at his home in New York City. The next day he was given the oath of office again in the Vice President's office in the Capitol by Chief Justice Morrison Waite.
Noteworthy: During the vice-presidential nomination which ultimately put Chester Arthur into the vice-presidency upon Garfield's death, eight nominating votes were cast for U.S. Senator Blanche K. Bruce from Mississippi. Senator Bruce was an African-American and this was the first time in American history that an African-American had received votes in a Presidential convention.
No inaugural speech.

GROVER CLEVELAND
(Democrat) Twenty-Second President

b. March 18, 1837 at Caldwell, New Jersey. He was born Steven Grover Cleveland, but later dropped the Stephen.

d. June 24, 1908 of "debility and old age" at age 71, in Princeton, N.J.

m. 1886, at age 49 to Frances Folsom, Two sons, three daughters.

Father: Rev. Richard F. Cleveland, a Presbyterian minister.

Prep School: Had to cease his schooling due to his father's death.

College: Read for the law.

Profession: Teacher at a school for the blind; lawyer; sheriff of Erie Co., N.Y.; Major of Buffalo, N.Y., Governor of N. Y.

Military Service: None.

Denomination: Presbyterian. He said, "I have always felt that my training as a minister's son has been more valuable to me as a strengthening influence than any other incident in my life."

President from: March 4, 1885 to March 4, 1889 (First term).

Inaugurated at: East Portico of the Capitol.

Sworn in by: Chief Justice Morrison Waite.

Bible used: The Bible his mother had given him years before.

Noteworthy: In his first election he won the popular vote by a margin of only 63,000 votes and was elected by the electoral college by a margin of 219 to 182. In his re-election bid he won the popular vote by a wider margin of 96,000 votes, but lost the electoral college, 223 to 168.

GROVER CLEVELAND
INAUGURAL ADDRESS AS THE 22ND PRESIDENT
WEDNESDAY, MARCH 4, 1885

Mr. Cleveland rode to the Capitol with President Arthur, who had taken office upon the assassination of President Garfield.

...Our duties are practical and call for industrious application, an intelligent perception of the claims of public office, and, above all, a firm determination, by united action, to secure to all the people of the land the full benefits of the best form of government ever vouchsafed to man. And let us not trust to human effort alone, but humbly acknowledging the power and goodness of Almighty God, who presides over the destiny of nations, and who has at all times been revealed in our country's history, let us invoke His aid and His blessings upon our labors.

BENJAMIN HARRISON
(Republican) Twenty-third President

b. August 20, 1833, at North Bend, Ohio.

d. March 13, 1901 of pneumonia, age 67.

m. 1853, Caroline Lavinia Scott, one son, one daughter. Caroline died 1892.

m. 1896, Mary Scott (Lord) Dimmick, one daughter (Mary was his first wife Caroline's, niece).

Father: John Scott Harrison, farmer and U.S. Congressman.

Grandfather: President William Henry Harrison.

Great-Grandfather: Benjamin Harrison, a signer of the Declaration of Independence.

Prep School: Home schooled, then to Farmer's College near Cincinnati.

College: Miami University at Oxford, Ohio.

Profession: Lawyer; Reporter for the Supreme Court of Indiana; Union soldier; one-term U.S. Senator.

Bar Membership: 1853, Ohio.

Military Service: Fought for the Union, began as Lt. of the 70th Indiana Volunteers, ended as a Brevet Brigadier General in 1865.

Denomination: Presbyterian. He believed that the purpose of all human activity is to serve God.

Church Service: Served first as a deacon then as an elder in his home church for 40 years. Taught Sunday School and Bible classes.

President from: March 4, 1889 to March 4, 1893.

Inaugurated at: East Portico of the Capitol .

Sworn in by: Chief Justice Melville Fuller.

Noteworthy: He was the only President to lose an election to the person he had defeated.

BENJAMIN HARRISON
INAUGURAL ADDRESS
MONDAY, MARCH 4, 1889

The Civil War veteran, jurist, and Senator from Indiana was the only grandson of a President to be elected to the office, as well as the only incumbent to lose in the following election to the person he had defeated. Recognizing the loneliness and responsibility of his lofty position, shortly after his inauguration he said, "Now I walk alone with God."

There is no constitutional or legal requirement that the President shall take the oath of office in the presence of the people, but there is so manifest an appropriateness in the public induction to office of the chief executive officer of the nation that from the beginning of the Government the people, to whose service the official oath consecrates the officer, have been called to witness the solemn ceremonial. The oath taken in the presence of the people becomes a mutual covenant...

...Entering thus solemnly into covenant with each other, we may reverently invoke and confidently expect the favor and help of Almighty God - that He will give to me wisdom, strength, and fidelity, and to our people a spirit of fraternity and a love of righteousness and peace...

...No other people have a government more worthy of their respect and love or a land so magnificent in extent, so pleasant to look upon, and so full of generous suggestion to enterprise and labor. God has placed upon our head a diadem and has laid at our feet power and wealth beyond definition or calculation. But we must not forget that we take these gifts upon the condition that justice and mercy shall hold the reins of power and that the upward avenues of hope shall be free to all the people...

...Each State will bring its generous contribution to the great aggregate of the nation's increase. And when the harvests from the fields, the cattle from the hills, and the ores of the earth shall have been weighed, counted, and valued, we will turn from them all to crown with the highest honor the State that has most promoted education, virtue, justice, and patriotism among its people.

GROVER CLEVELAND
(Democrat) Twenty-fourth President

See earlier entry: For his biographical material and First Inaugural address.

President from: March 4, 1893 to March 4, 1897.

Inaugurated at: East Portico of the Capitol.

Sworn in by: Chief Justice Melville Fuller.

Noteworthy: He won the popular vote all three times he ran for election, but won the electoral vote only twice.

His Inaugural Ball as the 24th President was the first to have electric lights.

GROVER CLEVELAND
INAUGURAL ADDRESS AS THE 24TH PRESIDENT
SATURDAY, MARCH 4, 1893

According to a ruling by the State Department, Grover Cleveland is both the 22nd and the 24thPresident, because his two terms were not consecutive, even though he was only the 22nd individual to hold the office of President.

...While every American citizen must contemplate with the utmost pride and enthusiasm the growth and expansion of our country, the sufficiency of our institutions to stand against the rudest shocks of violence, the wonderful thrift and enterprise of our people, and the demonstrated superiority of our free government, it behooves us to constantly watch for every symptom of insidious infirmity that threatens our national vigor...

...It can not be doubted that our stupendous achievements as a people and our country's robust strength have given rise to heedlessness of those laws governing our national health which we can no more evade than human life can escape the laws of God and nature...

...Under our scheme of government the waste of public money is a crime against the citizen, and the contempt of our people for economy and frugality in their personal affairs deplorably saps the strength and sturdiness of our national character.

It is a plain dictate of honesty and good government that public expenditures should be limited by public necessity, and that this should be measured by the rules of strict economy; and it is equally clear that frugality among the people is the best guaranty of a contented and strong support of free institutions...

The oath I now take to preserve, protect, and defend the Constitution of the United States not only impressively defines the great responsibility I assume, but suggests obedience to constitutional commands as the rule by which my official conduct must be guided...

...Above all, I know there is a Supreme Being who rules the affairs of men and whose goodness and mercy have always followed the American people, and I know He will not turn from us now if we humbly and reverently seek His powerful aid.

WILLIAM MCKINLEY
(Republican) Twenty-fifth President

b. January 29, 1843, at Niles, Ohio.

d. September 14, 1901, at Buffalo, age 58, from wounds inflicted by an assassin.

m. 1871, Ida Saxton, two daughters.

Father: William McKinley, an iron manufacturer.

Prep School: Poland Union Seminary, Poland, Ohio.

College: Allegheny College, Meadville, Pa.

Profession: School teacher; lawyer; Union soldier; served 15 years in Congress; two-term Ohio Governor.

Bar Membership: Ohio, 1867.

Military Service: Enlisted as a private in the Civil War at 18 years-old on June 1861. He ended the war as a major.

Church Denomination: Methodist, having professed his faith at a revival meeting at age 10.

Church Service: It was said that for thirty-five years he never failed to find a worship service on Sunday. He was Superintendent of the Sunday School at his home church.

President of the Young Men's Christian Association in Canton, Ohio, when the YMCA was truly an evangelistic outreach.

President: From March 4, 1897 to September 14, 1901.

First Inaugural: Inaugurated at North East Front steps at the Capitol.

Sworn in by: Chief Justice Melville Fuller.

His was the first inaugural recorded by Thomas Edison's new motion picture camera and the first inaugural address to be recorded by Thomas Edison's new gramophone.

Second Election: Inaugurated at the East Portico of the Capitol, and sworn in by Chief Justice Melville Fuller.

Noteworthy: Five months after his second inauguration, he was shot by an anarchist named Czolgosz, and died of the wounds 8 days later. His dying words were, "It is God's way."

WILLIAM MCKINLEY
FIRST INAUGURAL ADDRESS
THURSDAY, MARCH 4, 1897

At his inaugural he kissed the Bible which was opened to II Chronicles 1:10 "Give me now wisdom and knowledge, that I may go out and come in before the people: for who can judge this thy people, that is so great?"
Thomas Edison's new motion picture camera captured the inaugural events, and his gramophone recorded the address.

In obedience to the will of the people, and in their presence, by the authority vested in me by this oath, I assume the arduous and responsible duties of President of the United States, relying upon the support of my countrymen and invoking the guidance of Almighty God. Our faith teaches that there is no safer reliance than upon the God of our fathers, who has so singularly favored the American people in every national trial, and who will not forsake us so long as we obey His commandments and walk humbly in His footsteps...

...Illiteracy must be banished from the land if we shall attain that high destiny as the foremost of the enlightened nations of the world which,under Providence, we ought to achieve...

Let me again repeat the words of the oath administered by the Chief Justice which, in their respective spheres, so far as applicable, I would have all my countrymen observe: "I will faithfully execute the office of President of the United states, and will, to the best of my ability, preserve, protect, and defend the Constitution of the United States." This is the obligation I have reverently taken before the Lord Most High. To keep it will be my single purpose, my constant prayer.

WILLIAM MCKINLEY
SECOND INAUGURAL ADDRESS
MONDAY, MARCH 4, 1901

President McKinley again had defeated William Jennings Bryan. The new Vice President, Theodore Roosevelt, was a popular figure from the recent Spanish-American War.

...Intrusted by the people for a second time with the office of President, I enter upon its administration appreciating the great responsibilities which attach to this renewed honor and commission, promising unreserved devotion on my part to their faithful discharge and reverently invoking for my guidance the direction and favor of Almighty God.

Dark pictures and gloomy forebodings are worse than useless. These only becloud, they do not help to point the way of safety and honor. "Hope maketh not ashamed." The prophets of evil were not the builders of the Republic, nor in its crises since have they saved or served it. The faith of the fathers was a mighty force in its creation, and the faith of their descendants has wrought its progress and furnished its defenders...As heretofore, so hereafter will the nation demonstrate its fitness to administer any new estate which events devolve upon it, and in the fear of God will "take occasion by the hand and make the bounds of freedom wider yet."

THEODORE ROOSEVELT, JR.
(Republican) Twenty-sixth President

b. October 27, 1858, at New York City.

d. January 6, 1919 of rheumatism, age 60, at Sagamore Hill, Oyster Bay, New York.

m. 1883, Alice Hathaway Lee, one daughter. Alice died in 1884.

m. 1886, Edith Kermit Crow, four sons, one daughter.

Father: Theodore Roosevelt, sr., a glass importer and merchant.

Prep School: Homeschooled and tutored.

College: Harvard, attended Columbia Law School briefly.

Profession: Lawyer; rancher; author; Police Commissioner of New York; Civil Service Commissioner; Asst. Secretary of the Navy; Commander of the Rough Riders in Cuba; Governor of New York; Vice President.

Military Service: Commander of the Rough Riders in Cuba as a Lt. Col. for the 1st U.S. Vol. Calvary.

Denomination: Dutch Reformed

Church Service: Taught Sunday School at Christ's Church at Harvard until the Rector discovered he was not Episcopal.

President from: September 14, 1901 to March 4, 1909.

First Term: Inaugurated at the home of Ansley Wilcox on Delaware Avenue in Buffalon, New York.

No inaugural address

Second Term: Inaugurated at East Portico of the Capitol.

Sworn in by: Chief Justice Melville Fuller.

Noteworthy: His inaugural celebration reflected all of Roosevelt's diverse interests and all of America -- cowboys, Indians, coal miners, students, soldiers and more. He might have learned to appreciate cultural diversity at an early age: During the Civil War his father sent provisions to needy New Yorkers whose fathers and husbands were in the Union Army, while his loyal Southerner mother sent provisions back home to her needy friends and relatives who were fighting for the Confederacy.

After Taft's presidency, he left the Republican party and ran on the Progressive "Bull Moose" ticket. In doing so, the split of the Republican vote enabled Woodrow Wilson to win.

THEODORE ROOSEVELT
INAUGURAL ADDRESS
SATURDAY, MARCH 4, 1905

The energetic Republican President had taken his first oath of office upon the death of President McKinley, who died of an assassin's gunshot wounds on September 14, 1901. Mr. Roosevelt had been President himself for three years at the election of 1904. The inaugural celebration was the largest and most diverse of any in memory - cowboys, Indians (including the Apache Chief Geronimo), coal miners, soldiers, and students were some of the groups represented.

My fellow-citizens, no people on earth have more cause to be thankful than ours, and this is said reverently, in no spirit of boastfulness in our own strength, but with gratitude to the giver of Good who has blessed us with the conditions which have enabled us to achieve so large a measure of well-being and of happiness. To us as a people it has been granted to lay the foundations of our national life in a new continent...

Much has been given us, and much will rightfully be expected from us...Toward all other nations, large and small, our attitude must be one of cordial and sincere friendship. We must show not only in our words, but in our deeds, that we are earnestly desirous of securing their good will by acting toward them in a spirit of just and generous recognition of all their rights.

WILLIAM HOWARD TAFT
(Republican) Twenty-seventh President

b. September 15, 1857, in Cincinnati, Ohio.

d. March 8, 1930, of arteriosclerosis, in Washington, D.C.

m. 1886, Helen Herron, Two sons, one daughter.

Father: Alfonso Taft, Attorney General under Hayes.

Prep School: Woodward High School, Cincinnati, Ohio.

College: Yale University, Cincinnati Law School.

Military Service: None (although he served as Secretary of War).

Profession: Law Reporter for Cincinnati newspapers; Lawyer; Ass't Prosecutor and City Solicitor at Cincinnati; Superior Court Judge; Solicitor General of the U.S.; U.S. Circuit Court Judge; President, Philippine Commission; Governor of the Philippines; Secretary of War; Provisional Governor of Cuba; after being President, he was a professor of constitutional law until he was named the Chief Justice of the Supreme Court.

Denomination: Unitarian, "I believe in God," he said, "but I do not believe in the divinity of Christ. . . I am not, however, a scoffer at religion but on the contrary recognize, in the fullest manner, the elevating influence that it has had and always will have in the history of mankind."

President from: March 4, 1909 to March 4, 1913.

Inaugurated at: Senate Chamber in the Capitol (due to a blizzard).

Sworn in by: Chief Justice Melville Fuller.

Bible used: He took his oath on the Supreme Court Bible, which he used again in 1921 to take his oath as the Chief Justice of the Supreme Court.

WILLIAM HOWARD TAFT
INAUGURAL ADDRESS
THURSDAY, MARCH 4, 1909

A blizzard the night before caused the ceremonies to be moved into the Senate Chamber in the Capitol. The new President took his oath on the Supreme Court Bible, which he used again in 1921 to take his oaths as the Chief Justice of the Supreme Court.

Having thus reviewed the questions likely to recur during my administration, and having expressed in a summary way the position which I expect to take in recommendations to Congress and in my conduct as an Executive, I invoke the considerate sympathy and support of my fellow-citizens and the aid of the Almighty God in the discharge of my responsible duties.

THOMAS WOODROW WILSON
(Democrat) Twenty-eighth President

b. December 28, 1856, at Staunton, Virginia.

d. February 3, 1924 of heart disease at age 67, in Washington, D.C.

m. 1885, Ellen Louise Axson. Three daughters. She died in 1914.

m. 1915, Edith (Bolling) Galt.

Father: Rev. Joseph Ruggles Wilson, a Presbyterian minister.

Prep School: Mr. J. T. Derry's Academy, Augusta, Georgia. Homeschooled afterward by his father, a chaplain, and his maternal uncle, a teacher of evolution.

College: Davidson College, for a year, then at Princeton; University of Virginia Law School; Ph.D. Johns Hopkins University.

Profession: Lawyer; teacher; President of Princeton; Governor of New Jersey.

Military Service: None.

Denomination: Presbyterian. As President, he read the Bible daily, said grace before meals, and knelt to pray in the morning and at night.

Church Service: Elder of the Central Presbyterian Church in Washington. He said, "My life would not be worth living if it were not for the driving power of religion, for faith, pure and simple."

President: From March 4, 1913 to March 4, 1921.

First Election: Inaugurated at East Portico of the Capitol.

Sworn in by: Chief Justice Edward White.

Second Election: Inaugurated at the president's room in the Capitol by Chief Justice Edward White Sunday March 4, 1917.

Monday March 5, 1917, Inaugurated at the East Portico.

Sworn in by: Chief Justice Edward White.

Noteworthy: As a young scholar, "Tommy" Wilson wrote a friend that: "I find I need a trademark in advertising my literary wares. Thomas W. Wilson lacks something. Woodrow Wilson sticks in the mind. So I have decided publicly to be Woodrow Wilson."

Upon Wilson's election, the Senate, House of Representatives, President and Vice President were all Democratically controlled.

WOODROW WILSON
FIRST INAUGURAL ADDRESS
TUESDAY, MARCH 4, 1913

The election of 1912 produced a Democratic victory over the split vote for President Taft's Republican ticket and Theodore Roosevelt's Progressive ("Bull Moose") Party. With Wilson's election, the presidency, the House and the Senate were all Democratically-controlled.

There has been a change of government. It began two years ago, when the House of Representatives became Democratic by a decisive majority. It has now been completed. The Senate about to assemble will also be Democratic. The offices of President and Vice-president have been put into the hands of Democrats...

The nation has been deeply stirred, stirred by a solemn passion, stirred by the knowledge of wrong, of ideals lost, of government too often debauched and made an instrument of evil. The feelings with which we face this new age of right and opportunity sweep across our heartstrings like some air out of God's own presence, where justice and mercy are reconciled and the judge and the brother are one...

This is not a day of triumph; it is a day of dedication. Here muster, not the forces of party, but the forces of humanity. Men's hearts wait upon us; men's lives hang in the balance; men's hopes call upon us to say what we will do. Who shall live up to the great trust? Who dares fail to try? I summon all honest men, all patriotic, all forward-looking men, to my side. God helping me, I will not fail them, if they will but counsel and sustain me!

WOODROW WILSON
SECOND INAUGURAL ADDRESS
MONDAY, MARCH 5, 1917

March 4 was a Sunday, but the President took the oath of office at the Capitol in the President's Room that morning. The oath was publicly taken again the next day.

...We are being forged into a new unity amidst the fires that now blaze throughout the world. In their ardent heat we shall, in God's Providence, let us hope, be purged of faction and division, purified of the errant humors of party and of private interest, and shall stand forth in the days to come with a new dignity of national pride and spirit. Let each man see to it that the dedication is in his own heart, the high purpose of the nation in his own mind, ruler of his own will and desire...

...I know now what the task means. I realize to the full the responsibility which it involves. I pray God I may be given the wisdom and the prudence to do my duty in the true spirit of this great people. I am their servant and can succeed only as they sustain and guide me by their confidence and their counsel. The thing I shall count upon, the thing without which neither counsel nor action will avail, is the unity of America - an America united in feeling, in purpose and in its vision of duty, of opportunity and of service.

WARREN GAMALIEL HARDING
(Republican) Twenty-ninth President

b. November 2, 1865 at Corsica, (now called Blooming Grove) Ohio.

d. August 2, 1923 of pneumonia and heart trouble, age 57.

m. 1891, to Florence King. No children.

Father: Dr. George Harding, a physician and farmer.

Prep School: Occasional attendance at community schools.

College: Ohio Central College.

Profession: Began as a newspaper publisher at age 14; state senator; Lt. Governor of Ohio; U.S. Senator.

Military Service: None.

Denomination: Baptist.

Church Service: Trustee in his Baptist church in Marion, Ohio.

President from: March 4, 1921 to August 2, 1923.

Inaugurated at: The East Portico of the Capitol.

Sworn in by: Chief Justice Edward White.

Bible used: He was sworn in on the same Bible used by George Washington.

Noteworthy: Rode to the Capitol in the first automobile to be used in an inaugural. It was also the first inaugural to be broadcast to the crowd by a loud speaker.

He took ill while returning from a trip visiting the Territory of Alaska (which wanted statehood) and died in San Francisco.

WARREN G. HARDING
INAUGURAL ADDRESS
FRIDAY, MARCH 4, 1921

Senator Harding from Ohio was the first sitting Senator to be elected President. A former newspaper publisher and Governor of Ohio, the President-elect rode to the Capitol with President Wilson in the first automobile to be used in an inauguration. The oath of office was administered by Chief Justice Edward White, using the Bible from George Washington's first inauguration. The address to the crowd at the Captitol was the first to be broadcast on a loudspeaker.

...Standing in this presence, mindful of the solemnity of this occasion, feeling the emotions which no one may know until he senses the great weight of responsibility of himself, I must utter my belief in the divine inspiration of the founding fathers. Surely there must have been God's intent in the making of this new-world Republic. Ours is an organic law which had but one ambiguity, and we saw that effaced in a baptism of sacrifice and blood, with union maintained, the Nation supreme, and its concord inspiring. We have seen the world rivet its hopeful gaze on the great truths on which the founders wrought. We have seen civil, human, and religious liberty verified and glorified. In the beginning the Old World scoffed at our experiment; today our foundations of political and social belief stand unshaken, a precious inheritance to ourselves, an inspiring example of freedom and civilization to all mankind. Let us express renewed and strengthened devotion, in grateful reverence for the immortal beginning, and utter our confidence in the supreme fulfillment...

...America is ready to encourage, eager to initiate, anxious to participate in any seemly program likely to lessen the probability of war, and promote that brotherhood of mankind which must be God's highest conception of human relationship. Because we cherish ideals of justice and peace, because we appraise international comity and helpful relationship no less highly than any people of the world, we aspire to a high place in the moral leadership of civilization, and we hold a maintained America, the proven Republic, the unshaken temple of representative democracy, to be not only an inspiration and example, but the highest agency of strengthening good will and promoting accord on both continents...

..I wish for an America no less alert in guarding against dangers from within than it is watchful against enemies from without. Our fundamental law recognizes no class, no group, no section; there must be none in legislation or administration. The supreme inspiration is the common weal. Humanity hungers for international peace, and we crave it with all mankind. My most reverent prayer for America is for industrial peace, with its rewards, widely and general distributed, amid the inspirations of equal opportunity...

Service is the supreme commitment of life. I would rejoice to acclaim the era of the Golden Rule and crown it with the autocracy of service. I pledge an administration wherein all the agencies of Government are called to serve, and ever promote an understanding of Government purely as an expression of the popular will.

One cannot stand in this presence and be unmindful of the tremendous responsibility. The world upheaval has added heavily to our tasks. But with the realization comes the surge of high resolve, and there is reassurance in belief in the God-given destiny of our Republic. If I felt that there is to be sole responsibility in the Executive for the America of tomorrow I should shrink from the burden. But here are a hundred millions, with common concern and shared responsibility, answerable to God and country. The Republic summons them to their duty, and I invite co-operation.

I accept my part with single-mindedness of purpose and humility of spirit, and implore the favor and guidance of God in His Heaven. With these I am unafraid, and confidently face the future.

I have taken the solemn oath of office on that passage of Holy Writ wherein it is asked: "What doth the Lord require of thee but to do justly, and to love mercy, and to walk humbly with thy God?" This I plight to God and country.

CALVIN COOLIDGE
(Republican) Thirtieth President

b. July 4, 1872, at Plymouth, Vermont. He was born John Calvin Coolidge but dropped the use of his first name and registered as Calvin Coolidge when he went to Amherst.

d. January 5, 1933 of a sudden heart attack, in Northhampton, Massachusetts.

m. 1905, Grace A Goodhue. Two sons

Father: Col. John Calvin Coolidge, soldier, farmer, storekeeper.

Prep School: Neighborhood schools, then later Black River Academy, and St. Johnsbury Academy.

College: Amherst College in Northhampton, Massachusetts.

Profession: Lawyer; City Councilman; City Solicitor; Clerk of Courts; Mayor of Northhampton, Massachusetts.; State Senator; Lt. Gov.; Governor.

Military Service: None.

Denomination: Congregationalist.

President from: August 3, 1923 to March 4, 1929.

First Term: Inaugurated at the family sitting room of his father's farmhouse in Plymouth, Vermont.

Sworn in by: His father who was a notary.

No Inaugural Speech.

Second Term: Inaugurated at the East Portico of the Capitol.

Sworn in by: Chief Justice (and former President) William Howard Taft.

Noteworthy: He refused to be nominated by his party for a second elective office and said, "I do not choose to run for President in 1928."

Mr. Coolidge had a reputation for being a man of very few words. His wife told the story that one Sunday he returned home from worship at his Congregational church. Since she had not been able to attend, she asked him what the preacher's sermon was about. "Sin", answered Coolidge. His wife asked him what the preacher had said about it. "He was against it", replied the taciturn Coolidge.

CALVIN COOLIDGE
INAUGURAL ADDRESS
WEDNESDAY, MARCH 4, 1925

In 1923 President Coolidge first took the oath of office, adminis- tered by his father, a justice of the peace and a notary, in his family's sit- ting room in Plymouth, Vermont. President Harding had died while trav- eling in the western States. A year later, the President was elected on the slogan "Keep Cool with Coolidge." The event was broadcast to the nation by radio.

...If we wish to erect new structures, we must have a definite knowledge of the old foundations. We must realize that human nature is about the most constant thing in the universe and that the essentials of human relationship do not change...

...We have been, and propose to be, more and more American. We believe that we can best serve our own country and most successfully discharge our obligations to humanity by continuing to be openly and can- didly, intensely and scrupulously, American. If we have any heritage, it has been that. If we have any destiny, we have found it in that direction.

But if we wish to continue to be distinctively American, we must continue to make that term comprehensive enough to embrace the legiti- mate desires of a civilized and enlightened people determined in all their relations to pursue a conscientious and religious life...

...Conditions must be provided under which people can make a living and work out of their difficulties. But there is another element, more important than all, without which there can not be the slightest hope of a permanent peace. That element lies in the heart of humanity. Unless the desire for peace be cherished there, unless this fundamental and only natural source of brotherly love be cultivated to its highest degree, all arti- ficial efforts will be in vain. Peace will come when there is realization that only under a reign of law, based on righteousness and supported by the religious conviction of the brotherhood of man, can there be any hope of a complete and satisfying life. Parchment will fail, the sword will fail, it is only the spiritual nature of man that can be triumphant...

...It would be well if we could replace much that is only a false and ignorant prejudice with a true and enlightened pride of race. But the last election showed that appeals to class and nationality had little effect. We were all found loyal to a common citizenship. The fundamental precept of liberty is toleration We can not permit any inquisition either within or without the law or apply any religious test to the holding of office. The mind of America must be forever free...

The past and present show faith and hope and courage fully justified. Here stands our country, an example of tranquillity at home, a patron of tranquillity abroad. Here stands its Government, aware of its might but obedient to its conscience. Here it will continue to stand, seeking peace and prosperity, solicitous for the welfare of the wage earner, promoting enterprise, developing waterways and natural resources, attentive to the intuitive counsel of womanhood, encouraging education, desireing the advancement of religion, supporting the cause of justice and honor among the nations. America seeks no earthly empire built on blood and force. No ambition, no temptation, lures her to thought of foreign dominions. The legions which she sends forth are armed, not with the sword, but with the cross. The higher state to which she seeks the allegiance of all mankind is not of human, but of divine origin. She cherishes no purpose save to merit the favor of Almighty God.

HERBERT CLARK HOOVER
(Republican) Thirty-first President

b. August 10, 1874, at West Branch, Iowa.

d. Oct. 20, 1964, in N.Y.C., N.Y.

m. 1899 to Lou Henry. Two sons.

Father: Jesse Clark Hoover, a blacksmith, died when struck by a falling tree when Hoover was six. His mother, who was a minister in her Quaker church, died when Hoover was nine years old.

Prep School: After being orphaned, he lived with three different uncles, had sporadic schooling the last of which was at the Pacific Academy (currently George Fox College) where one of his uncles was superintendent.

College: Stanford University.

Profession: Mining Engineer; United States Food Administrator; Secretary of Commerce. He held no elective office before the Presidency.

Military Service: None, Hoover was a pacifist.

Denomination: Quaker. By age 10, he had read the entire Bible. As President, he attended the Friends Meeting House in Washington.

Church Service: While Chief Engineer of the Imperial Mines in China, he directed the relief effort for victims of the Boxer Rebellion. During WWI, he directed the American Relief Committee in London. Later he directed relief efforts for the U.S. Committee for Relief in Belgium, and Russia.

President from: March 4, 1929 to March 4, 1933.

Inaugurated at: The East Portico of the Capitol.

Sworn in by: Chief Justice (and former President) William Howard Taft. As part of the inaugural celebrations, dirigibles and aircraft flew over the Capitol.

Noteworthy: His work in relief efforts perfectly prepared him to be President during the era of the Great Depression.

HERBERT HOOVER
INAUGURAL ADDRESS
MONDAY, MARCH 4, 1929

Dirigibles and aircraft flew over the Capitol to mark the occasion.

This occasion is not alone the administration of the most sacred oath which can be assumed by an American citizen, It is a dedication and consecration under God to the highest office in service of our people. I assume this trust in the humility of knowledge that only through the guidance of Almighty Providence can I hope to discharge its ever-increasing burdens...

...Ours is a land rich in resources; stimulating in its glorious beauty; filled with millions of happy homes; blessed with comfort and opportunity. In no nation are the institutions of progress more advanced. In no nation are the fruits of accomplishment more secure. In no nation is the government more worthy of respect. No country is more loved by its people. I have an abiding faith in their capacity, integrity and high purpose. I have no fears for the future of our country. It is bright with hope.

In the presence of my countrymen, mindful of the solemnity of this occasion, knowing what the task means and the responsibility which it involves, I beg your tolerance, your aid, and your cooperation. I ask the help of Almighty God in this service to my country to which you have called me.

FRANKLIN DELANO ROOSEVELT
(Democrat) Thirty-second President

b. January 30, 1882, Hyde Park, New York.

d. April 12, 1945, at Warm Springs, Georgia.

m. 1905, Anna Eleanor Roosevelt, a fourth cousin. Anna was also the niece of the then current president, Theodore Roosevelt, who gave her in marriage to FDR. Five sons, one daughter.

Father: James Roosevelt, capitalist and landholder.

(FDR was a fifth cousin to Theodore Roosevelt.)

Prep School: Homeschooled by private tutors and French and German governesses. Entered Groton School at age 14. (The philosophy of Groton was "Each crown carries a cross.")

College: Harvard University; Columbia University Law School.

Profession: Lawyer; New York State Senator; Ass't Secretary of the Navy; vice president of Fidelity and Deposit Co.; unsuccessful U.S. Vice Presidential candidate in 1920; two-term Governor of New York.

Military Service: None.

Denomination: Episcopalian.

Church Service: Vestryman and Senior Warden of his home church.

President from: March 4, 1933 to April 12, 1945.

First Term: Inaugurated at the East Portico of the Capitol.

Sworn in by: Chief Justice Charles Evans Hughes.

Vice President: John Nance Garner of Texas.

Second Term: Inaugurated at the East Portico of the Capitol.

Sworn in by: Chief Justice Charles Evans Hughes.

For the first time the inauguration of the President was held on January 20, pursuant to the newly passed 20th Amendment to the Constitution.

Vice President: John Nance Garner of Texas.

Third Term: Inaugurated at the East Portico on the Capitol.

Sworn in by: Chief Justice Charles Evans Hughes.

Vice President: Henry Wallace.

Fourth Term: Inaugurated at the South Portico of the White House.

Sworn in by: Chief Justice Harlan Stone.

Vice President: Harry S. Truman of Missouri.

Noteworthy: FDR was the only President to serve more than two terms. Before FDR, all presidents followed the tradition set by George Washington of declining to serve more than two terms. After FDR, the 22nd Amendment to the Constitution was passed which prevented any president from ever again serving more than two elected terms of office.

FRANKLIN D. ROOSEVELT
FIRST INAUGURAL ADDRESS
SATURDAY, MARCH 4, 1933

Roosevelt's first Inauguration Day was cold, rainy and gray. Immediately upon taking office, FDR issued an emergency order temporarily closing all the banks in the nation. A little more than a month after taking office, on April 19 he abandoned the monetary gold standard.

Other items passed or decreed during his "First 100 Days" were a national relief system; a national farm policy; the Emergency Farm Mortgage Act, and other sweeping changes. During the campaign, President Hoover had said that Roosevelt and his supporters were "exponents of a social philosophy different from the traditional American one".

...This great Nation will endure as it has endured, will revive and will prosper...

...In such a spirit on my part and on yours we face our common difficulties. They concern, thank God, only material things...

...We face the arduous days that lie before us in the warm courage of the national unity; with the clear consciousness of seeking old and precious moral values; with the clean satisfaction that comes from the stem performance of duty by old and young alike. We aim at the assurance of a rounded and permanent national life.

We do not distrust the future of essential democracy. The people of the United States have not failed. In their need they have registered a mandate that they want direct, vigorous action. They have asked for discipline and direction under leadership. They have made me the present instrument of their wishes. In the spirit of the gift I take it.

In this dedication of a Nation we humbly ask the blessing of God. May He protect each and every one of us. May He guide me in the days to come.

FRANKLIN D. ROOSEVELT
SECOND INAUGURAL ADDRESS
WEDNESDAY, JANUARY 20, 1937

For the first time the inauguration of the President was held on January, 20, pursuant to the provisions of the 20th amendment to the constitution. A steady, cold rain drummed down on the top-hatted heads of those assembled for the inauguration.

A poll taken at the election's end found that only 15% of the people wanted a "more liberal" administration than the last, while 50% hoped that FDR would become "more conservative."

...In taking again the oath of office as President of the United States, I assume the solemn obligation of leading the American people forward along the road over which they have chosen to advance.

While this duty rests upon me I shall do my utmost to speak their purpose and to do their will, seeking Divine guidance to help us each and every one to give light to them that sit in darkness and to guide our feet into the way of peace.

FRANKLIN D. ROOSEVELT
THIRD INAUGURAL ADDRESS
MONDAY, JANUARY 20, 1941

The only chief executive to serve more than two terms, President Roosevelt took office for the third time as Europe and Asia engaged in war. Two weeks earlier, Roosevelt had given his "Four Freedoms" speech to Congress and asked them to give millions in Aid to other nations who were fighting Nazi Germany.

On each national day of inauguration since 1789, the people have renewed their sense of dedication to the United States.

In Washington's day the task of the people was to create and weld together a nation.

In Lincoln's day the task of the people was to preserve that Nation from disruption from within.

In this day the task of the people is to save that Nation and its institutions from disruption from without.

..In the face of great perils never before encountered, our strong purpose is to protect and to perpetuate the integrity of democracy.

For this we muster the spirit of America, and the faith of America.

We do not retreat. We are not content to stand still. As Americans, we go forward, in the service of our country, by the will of God.

FRANKLIN D. ROOSEVELT
FOURTH INAUGURAL ADDRESS
SATURDAY, JANUARY 20, 1945

The fourth inauguration was conducted without fanfare. No formal celebrations followed the address. Instead of renominating Vice President Henry Wallace in the election of 1944, the Democratic convention chose the Senator from Missouri, Harry S. Truman. Three months later, President Roosevelt died of a cerebral hemorrhage at "the Little White House" in Warm Springs, Georgia.

...We Americans of today, together with our allies, are passing through a period of supreme test. It is a test of our courage - of our resolve - of our wisdom - our essential democracy...

...As I stand here today, having taken the solemn oath of office in the presence of my fellow countrymen - in the presence of our God - I know that it is America's purpose that we shall not fail...

...We can gain no lasting peace if we approach it with suspicion and mistrust or with fear. We can gain it only if we proceed with the understanding, the confidence, and the courage which flow from conviction.

The Almighty God has blessed our land in many ways. He has given our people stout hearts and strong arms with which to strike mighty blows for freedom and truth. He has given to our country a faith which has become the hope of all peoples in an anguished world.

So we pray to Him now for the vision to see our way clearly - to see the way that leads to a better life for ourselves and for all our fellow men - to the achievement of His will to peace on earth.

HARRY S TRUMAN
(Democrat) Thirty-third President

b. May 8th, 1884, Lamar, Missouri.

d. Dec. 26, 1972, in Kansas City, Missouri.

m. Elizabeth V. "Bess" Wallace. One daughter, (Mary) Margaret.

Father: John Anderson Truman, Farmer and livestock dealer.

Prep School: Began 1st grade at age 8 at Noland School in Independence; Columbian School; Ott School; received evening tutoring with Miss Margaret Phelps to prepare for entry to West Point or Annapolis.

College: Rejected by West Point and Annapolis because of bad eyesight; attended but did not graduate from night classes at Kansas City Law School.

Profession: Railroad timekeeper; newspaper mailroom worker; bank clerk; bookkeeper; farmer; soldier; haberdashery owner; County Judge; partner in a Savings and Loan Ass'n, membership salesman for Automobile Club of Missouri; U.S. Senator two terms.

Military Service: Joined National Guard in 1905 as a private; active duty in W.W.I, began as a First Lieutenant and mustered out as a Major in 1919; organized the First Reserve Officers Association in the U.S.

Denomination: Attended Presbyterian church as a child; attended First Baptist Church as President because "the preacher always treats me as a church member and not as the head of a circus." He proclaimed July 4, 1952, the first annual day of prayer.

President from: April 12, 1945 to January 19, 1953.

First term: Sworn in at 9:07 p.m., April 12, 1945, by Chief Justice Harlan Stone in the White House with his wife Bess and daughter Margaret in attendance.

Bible used: One which Truman found in a White House bookcase.

No Inaugural Speech.

Second Term: Inaugurated at the East Portico of the Capitol.

The inaugural was televised as far West as Sedalia, Missouri and broadcast on the radio.

Bible used: He took the oath of office on two Bibles; the personal one he had used for his first oath and a Gutenberg Bible donated by the citizens of Independence, Missouri.

Noteworthy: The reason he only used the initial "S" for his middle name was because there was a family disagreement over whether his middle name was Shippe or Solomon, after the names of two grandfathers.

HARRY S. TRUMAN
INAUGURAL ADDRESS
THURSDAY, JANUARY 20, 1949

A former county judge, Senator and Vice President, Harry S. Truman had taken the oath of office first on April 12, 1945, upon the death of President Roosevelt. Mr. Truman's victory in the 1948 election was so unexpected that many newspapers had declared the Republican candidate, Governor Thomas E. Dewey of New York, the winner. The President went to the East Portico of the Capitol to take the oath of office on two Bibles-the personal one he had used for the first oath, and a Gutenberg Bible donated by the citizens of Independence, Missouri. The ceremony was televised and broadcast on the radio. Ten million people witnessed this inauguration--many more than the combined total of all the previous inaugurations.

Mr. Vice President, Mr. Chief Justice, and fellow citizens, I accept with humility the honor which the American people have conferred upon me...

In performing the duties of my office, I need the help and prayers of every one of you. I ask for your encouragement and your support. The tasks we face are difficult, and we can accomplish them only if we work together.

...The supreme need of our time is for men to learn to live together in peace and harmony.

The peoples of the earth face the future with grave uncertainty, composed almost equally of great hopes and great fears. In this time of doubt, they look to the United States as never before for good will, strength, and wise leadership.

It is fitting, therefore, that we take this occasion to proclaim to the world the essential principles of the faith by which we live, and to declare our aims to all peoples.

The American people stand firm in the faith which has inspired this Nation from the beginning. We believe that all men have a right to equal justice under law and equal opportunity to share in the common good. We believe that all men have the right to freedom of thought and expression. We believe that all men are created equal because they are created in the image of God.

From this faith we will not be moved.

The American people desire, and are determined to work for, a world in which all nations and all peoples are free to govern themselves as they see fit, and to achieve a decent and satisfying life. Above all else, our people desire, and are determined to work for, peace on earth--a just and lasting peace--based on genuine agreement freely arrived at by equals.

In the pursuit of these aims, the United States and other like-minded nations find themselves directly opposed by a regime with contrary aims and a totally different concept of life.

That regime adheres to a false philosophy which purports to offer freedom, security, and greater opportunity to mankind...

That false philosophy is communism.

Communism is based on the belief that man is so weak and inadequate that he is unable to govern himself, and therefore requires the rule of strong masters.

Democracy is based on the conviction that man has the moral and intellectual capacity, as well as the inalienable right, to govern himself with reason and justice.

...These differences between communism and democracy do not concern the United States alone. People everywhere are coming to realize that what is involved is material well-being, human dignity, and the right to believe in and worship God...

...Events have brought our American democracy to new influence and new responsibilities. They will test our courage, our devotion to duty, and our concept of liberty.

But I say to all men, what we have achieved in liberty, we will surpass in greater liberty.

Steadfast in our faith in the Almighty, we will advance toward a world where man's freedom is secure.

To that end we will devote our strength, our resources, and our firmness of resolve. With God's help, the future of mankind will be assured in a world of justice, harmony, and peace.

DWIGHT DAVID "IKE" EISENHOWER
(Republican) Thirty-fourth President

b. Oct. 14, 1890 Denison, Texas, birth name was David Dwight Eisenhower, but he reversed the order to Dwight David when he went to West Point.

d. March 28, 1969, in Washington, D.C.

m. 1916 Mary G. "Mamie" Doud, Two sons, one of whom died as an infant.

Father: David Jacob Eisenhower, mechanic at a creamery in Abilene, Kansas.

Prep School: Public schools in Abilene, Kansas.

College: Applied to the Naval Academy but was rejected as too old, later accepted at West Point.

Profession: Soldier. Began as a 2nd Lt. in Ft. Sam Houston, TX.; served stateside in W.W.I, commanding the tank training center at Gettysburg, PA.; served under Pershing and McArthur during peacetime; named Ass't Chief of Staff in 1942; later that year became Comdr. European Theater of Operations; 1943, Supreme Allied Comdr. in Europe; 1944, led D-Day invasion of France; 1945 General of the Army; 1945 Army Chief of Staff; President of Columbia College, 1948-1950; Commanded NATO at Truman's request, 1950-1952.

Denomination: Raised in the River Brethren faith as a child but baptized as an adult as a Presbyterian. He began the White House Prayer Breakfast and opened Cabinet meetings with prayer.

President from: January 20, 1953 to January 19, 1961.

(Both parties tried to draft him in 1948)

First Term: Sworn in by Chief Justice Frederick Vinson.

Bible used: He used two; the one used by George Washington at the first inauguration, and the one his mother gave him when he graduated from West Point.

Second term: inaugurated at: East Portico of the Capitol on January 21, 1957,(January 20th occurred on a Sunday so he was privately sworn in that day in the East Room of the White House). Sworn in by Chief Justice Earl Warren.

Bible used: The one his mother gave him when he graduated from West Point.

DWIGHT D. EISENHOWER
FIRST INAUGURAL ADDRESS
TUESDAY, JANUARY 20, 1953

The Republican Party successfully promoted the candidacy of the popular General of the Army in the 1952 election over the Democratic candidate, Adlai Stevenson. The oath of office was administered by Chief Justice Frederick Vinson on two Bibles - the one used by George Washington at the first inauguration, and the one General Eisenhower received from his mother upon his graduation from the Military Academy at West Point. Twenty-one million homes from New York to California watched this first coast-to-coast broadcast of a presidential inauguration.

My friends, before I begin the expression of those thoughts that I deem appropriate to this moment, would you permit me the privilege of uttering a little private prayer of my own. And I ask that you bow your heads:

Almighty God, as we stand here at this moment my future associates in the executive branch of government join me in beseeching that Thou will make full and complete our dedication to the service of the people in this throng, and their fellow citizens everywhere.

Give us, we pray, the power to discern clearly right from wrong, and allow all our words and actions to be governed thereby, and by the laws of this land. Especially we pray that our concern shall be for all the people regardless of station, race, or calling.

May cooperation be permittted and be the mutual aim of those who, under the concepts of our Constitution, hold to differing political faiths; so that all may work for the good of our beloved country and Thy glory. Amen.

My fellow citizens:

...We are summoned by this honored and historic ceremony to witness more than the act of one citizen swearing his oath of service, in the presence of God. We are called as a people to give testimony in the sight of the world to our faith that the future shall belong to the free.

Since this century's beginning, a time of tempest has seemed to come upon the continents of the earth...

...In the swift rush of great events, we find ourselves groping to know the full sense and meaning of these times in which we live. In our quest of understanding, we beseech God's guidance. We summon all our knowledge of the past and we scan all sights of the future. We bring all our wit and all our will to meet the question:

How far have we come in man's long pilgrimage from darkness toward light: Are we nearing the light - a day of freedom and of peace for all mankind? Or are the shadows of another night closing in upon us?...

...At such a time in history, we who are free must proclaim anew our faith. This faith is the abiding creed of our fathers. It is our faith in the deathless dignity of man, governed by eternal moral and natural laws.

This faith defines our full view of life. It establishes, beyond debate, those gifts of the Creator that are man's inalienable rights, and that make all men equal in His sight.

In the light of this equality, we know that the virtues most cherished by free people - love of truth, pride of work, devotion to country - all are treasures equally precious in the lives of the most humble and of the most exalted. The men who mine coal and fire furnaces and balance ledgers and turn lathes and pick cotton and heal the sick and plant corn - all serve as proudly, and as profitably, for America as the statesmen who draft treaties and the legislators who enact laws.

This faith rules our whole way of life. It decrees that we, the people, elect leaders not to rule but to serve. It asserts that we have the right to choice of our own work and to the reward of our own toil. It inspires the initiative that makes our productivity the wonder of the world. And it warns that any man who seeks to deny equality among all his brothers betrays the spirit of the free and invites the mockery of the tyrant.

It is because we, all of us, hold to these principles that the political changes accomplished this day do not imply turbulence, upheaval or disorder. Rather this change expresses a purpose of strengthening our dedication and devotion to the precepts of our founding documents, a conscious renewal of faith in our country and in the watchfulness of a Divine Providence.

The enemies of this faith know no god but force, no devotion but its use. They tutor men in treason. They feed upon the hunger of others. Whatever defies them, they torture, especially the truth.

Here, then, is joined no argument between slightly differing philosophies. This conflict strikes directly at the faith of our fathers and the lives of our sons. No principle or treasure that we hold, from the spiritual knowledge of our free schools and churches to the creative magic of free labor and capital, nothing lies safely beyond the reach of this struggle.

Freedom is pitted against slavery; lightness against the dark...

...We feel this moral strength because we know that we are not helpless prisoners of history. We are free men. We shall remain free, never to be proven guilty of the one capital offense against freedom, a lack of stanch faith...

...Moral stamina means more energy and more productivity, on the farm and in the factory. Love of liberty means the guarding of every resource that makes freedom possible - from the sanctity of our families and the wealth of our soil to the genius of our scientists...

...The peace we seek, then, is nothing less than the practice and fulfillment of our whole faith among ourselves and in our dealings with others. This signifies more than the stilling of guns, casing the sorrow of war. More than escape from death, it is a way of life. More than a haven for the wary, it is a hope for the brave.

This is the hope that beckons us onward in this century of trial. This is the work that awaits us all, to be done with bravery, with charity, and with prayer to Almighty God.

DWIGHT D. EISENHOWER
SECOND INAUGURAL ADDRESS
MONDAY, JANUARY 21, 1957

January 20 occurred on a Sunday, so the President took the oath in the East Room at the White House that morning. The next day he repeated the oath of office on the East Portico of the Capitol. Chief Justice Earl Warren administered the oath of office on the President's personal Bible he had received from his mother upon graduation from West Point. Marian Anderson sang at the ceremony at the Capitol.

...Before all else, we seek, upon our common labor as a nation, the blessings of Almighty God. And the hopes in our hearts fashion the deepest prayers of our whole people.

May we pursue the right - without self-righteousness.

May we know unity - without conformity.

May we grow in strength - without pride in self.

May we, in our dealings with all peoples of the earth, ever speak truth and serve justice...

JOHN FITZGERALD KENNEDY
(Democrat) Thirty-fifth President

b. May 29, 1917, in Brookline, Mass.

d. November 22, 1963 in Dallas, Texas by an assassin's bullet.

m. 1953, Jacqueline Lee Bouvier; one daughter; two sons; one of whom died shortly after birth.

Father: Joseph P. Kennedy, businessman and financier, S.E.C. Chairman, Ambassador to Great Britain.

Prep School: Public elementary schools, then to Canterbury School in Milford, Conn., then to Choate in Wallingford, Connecticut.

College: Entered but quickly left Princeton due to health; graduated from Harvard, B.S. in political science; attended Stanford University Business School for 6 months.

Profession: Sailor; reporter for Hearst newspapers; U.S. House of Representatives three terms; Twice elected U.S. Senator.

Military: U.S. Navy, began as ensign; commanded a motor torpedo patrol boat (PT-109) in the Solomon Islands. Finished W.W.II as a Lt.

Denomination: Catholic.

President from: January 20, 1961 to November 22, 1963.

Inaugurated at: The expanded East Front of the Capitol.

Sworn in by: Chief Justice Earl Warren.

Noteworthy: Kennedy's was the first presidential campaign that had televised debates.

He was the youngest man ever elected president and the youngest to die in office.

JOHN F. KENNEDY
INAUGURAL ADDRESS
FRIDAY, JANUARY 20, 1961

Heavy snow fell the night before the inauguration, but thoughts about cancelling the plans were overruled. Mr. Kennedy attended Holy Trinity Catholic Church in Georgetown that morning before joining President Eisenhower to travel to the Capitol.

...[W]e observe today not a victory of party, but a celebration of freedom - symbolizing an end, as well as a beginning - signifying renewal, as well as change. For I have sworn before you and Almighty God the same solemn oath our forebears prescribed nearly a century and three quarters ago.

The world is very different now. For man holds in his mortal hands the power to abolish all forms of human poverty and all forms of human life. And yet the same revolutionary beliefs for which our forebears fought are still at issue around the globe - the belief that the rights of man come not from the generosity of the state, but from the hand of God.

We dare not forget today that we are the heirs of that first revolution. Let the word go forth from this time and place, to friend and foe alike, that the torch has been passed to a new generation of Americans - born in this century, tempered by war, disciplined by a hard and bitter peace, proud of our ancient heritage - and unwilling to witness or permit the slow undoing of those human rights to which this nation has always been committed, and to which we are committed today at home and around the world.

...Let both sides unite to heed in all corners of the earth the command of Isaiah - to "Undo the heavy burdens...and to let the oppressed go free"...

...In the long history of the world, only a few generations have been granted the role of defending freedom in its hour of maximum danger. I do not shank from this responsibility - I welcome it. I do not believe that any of us would exchange places with any other people or any other generation. The energy, the faith, the devotion which we bring to this endeavor will light our country and all who serve it - and the glow from that fire can truly light the world.

And so, my fellow Americans: ask not what your country can do for you - ask what you can do for you country.

My fellow citizens of the world: ask not what America will do for you, but what together we can do for the freedom of man.

Finally, whether you are citizens of America or citizens of the world, ask of us the same high standards of strength and sacrifice which we ask of you. With a good conscience our only sure reward, with history the final judge of our deeds, let us go forth to lead the land we love, asking His blessing and His help, but knowing that here on earth God's work must truly be our own.

LYNDON BAINES JOHNSON
(Democrat) Thirty-sixth President

b. Aug. 27, 1908, in the Texas hill country near Stonewall, Texas.

d. Jan. 22, 1973, at the LBJ Ranch.

m. Claudia Alta "Lady Bird" Taylor: two daughters.

Father: Sam Ealy Johnson, real estate, newspaperman and State politician.

Prep School: Johnson City High School.

College: Southwest Texas State Teachers College, San Marcos, Texas; attended but did not graduate from Georgetown University Law School.

Profession: Elevator operator; car washer; field hand; teacher; school principal; Director of National Youth Administration in Texas; 6 terms in U.S. House of Representatives; 2 terms in U.S. Senate; Vice President.

Military: Served as U.S.N. Lt. Comdr. for 7 months after Pearl Harbor until FDR recalled all Congressmen from Active Duty.

Denomination: Disciples of Christ. After Kennedy's assasination, he regularly said grace at meals and prayed often. He and daughter Luci privately held a prayer vigil one night at St. Dominic's Chapel over a concern of the Soviets entering the Vietnam War.

President from: November 22, 1963 to January 20, 1969.

First term inaugurated: On Board the Air Force One, the Presidential jet in Dallas, 98 minutes after the death of President Kennedy. Jacqueline Kennedy stood beside Johnson as he read the 34 word oath, still wearing the stockings and skirt which were splattered with her husband's blood. Four hours later he was in Washington, D.C. and made a public statement to the country which ended, "I will do my best. That is all I can do. I ask for your help -- and God's."

Second term: Inaugurated at the East Front of the Capitol on January 20, 1965.

Sworn in by: Chief Justice Earl Warren.

Noteworthy: At this inauguration, Mrs. Johnson joined the President on the platform, the first wife to stand with her husband at a formal inauguration as he took the oath of office.

LYNDON BAINES JOHNSON
INAUGURAL ADDRESS
WEDNESDAY, JANUARY 20, 1965

President Johnson had first taken the oath of office on board Air Force One on November 22, 1963, the day President Kennedy was assassinated in Dallas. At his second oath, after the landslide 1964 victory, Mrs. Johnson was the first wife to stand with her husband at a formal inauguration as he took the oath of office.

My fellow countrymen, on this occasion, the oath I have taken before you and before God is not mine alone, but ours together. We are one nation and one people. Our fate as a nation and our future as a people rest not upon one citizen, but upon all citizens...

Our destiny in the midst of change will rest on the unchanged character of our people, and on their faith.

They came here - the exile and the stranger, brave but frightened - to find a place where a man could be his own man. They made a covenant with this land. Conceived in justice, written in liberty, bound in union, it was meant one day to inspire the hopes of all mankind; and it binds us still. If we keep its terms, we shall flourish...

...Under this covenant of justice, liberty, and union we have become a nation - prosperous, great, and mighty. And we have kept our freedom. But we have no promise from God that our greatness will endure. We have been allowed by Him to seek greatness with the sweat of our hands and the strength of our spirit...

...If we fail now, we shall have forgotten in abundance what we learned in hardship; that democracy rests on faith, that freedom asks more than it gives, and that the judgment of God is harshest on those who are most favored...

...For myself, I ask only, in the words of an ancient leader: "Give me now wisdom and knowledge, that I may go out and come in before this people: for who can judge this thy people, that is so great?"

RICHARD MILHOUS NIXON
(Republican) Thirty seventh President

b. Jan. 9, 1913, in Yorba Linda, California.

d. April 22, 1994, age 81, in New York City.

m. 1940, (Thelma C.) Patricia "Pat" Ryan; two daughters.

Father: Francis Anthony Nixon, a Methodist who converted to the Quaker faith of his wife, citrus grower and a gas station-grocery operator.

Prep School: Whittier Union High.

College: Whittier College, A Quaker institution; Duke University Law School

Profession: Bean picker; janitor; barker at an amusement park; lawyer; co-owner of orange juice company; assistant city attorney; Naval officer; U.S. House of Representatives, 2 terms; U.S. Senate; Vice President.

Military: Even though eligible for conscientious-objector status, he enlisted in the U.S. Navy as a Lt. j.g., ended as a Lt. Cmndr.

Denomination: Quaker.

President from: January 20, 1969 to January 20, 1977.

First Term Inaugurated at: East Front of the Capitol.

Sworn in by: For the fifth and last time Chief Justice Earl Warren administered the inaugural oath.

The inaugural address was televised by satellite around the world.

Second term inaugurated at: East Front of the Capitol.

Sworn in by: Chief Justice Warren Burger.

Noteworthy: Won his first election by one of the closest votes in U.S. history.

With 60.7% of the voters going for Nixon, he won his second election with the largest number of popular votes in U. S. history. Cumulatively, he won more votes for president than any other American in history, having won 113,063, 548 votes in three elections.

A friend mentioned to him that he would probably be most noted by historians because of his opening to China. Ex-president Nixon disagreed, saying: "Historians are more likely to lead with 'He resigned from office.' " Mr. Nixon is the only U.S. President to have resigned from office.

RICHARD MILHOUS NIXON
FIRST INAUGURAL ADDRESS
MONDAY, JANUARY 20, 1969

An almost-winner of the 1960 election, and a close winner of the 1968 election, the former Vice President and California Senator and Congressman had defeated the Democratic Vice President, Hubert Humphrey, and the American Independent Party candidate, George Wallace. Chief Justice Earl Warren administered the oath of office for his fifth and last time. The President addressed the large crowd from a pavilion on the East Front of the Capitol. The address was televised by satellite around the world.

...Standing in this same place a third of a century ago, Franklin Delano Roosevelt addressed a Nation ravaged by depression and gripped in fear. He could say in surveying the Nation's troubles: "They concern, thank God, only material things."

Our crisis today is the reverse.

We have found ourselves rich in goods, but ragged in spirit; reaching with magnificent precision for the moon, but falling into raucous discord on earth.

...To a crisis of the spirit, we need an answer of the spirit.

To find that answer, we need only look within ourselves.

When we listen to "the better angels of our nature." we find that they celebrate the simple things, the basic things - such as goodness, decency, love, kindness...

...No man can be fully free while his neighbor is not. To go forward at all is to go forward together.

This means black and white together, as one nation, not two. The laws have caught up with our conscience   What remains is to give life to what is in the law: to ensure at last that as all are born equal in dignity before God, all are born equal in dignity before man...

...I have taken an oath today in the presence of God and my countrymen to uphold and defend the Constitution of the United States. To that oath I now add this sacred commitment: I shall consecrate my office, my energies, and all the wisdom I can summon, to the cause of peace among nations.

...Only a few short weeks ago, we shared the glory of man's first sight of the world as God sees it, as a single sphere reflecting light in the darkness.

As the Apollo astronauts flew over the moon's gray surface on Christmas Eve, they spoke to us of the beauty of earth - and in that voice so clear across the lunar distance, we heard them invoke God's blessing on its goodness...

...We have endured a long night of the American spirit. But as our eyes catch the dimness of the first rays of dawn, let us not curse the remaining dark. Let us gather the light.

Our destiny offers, not the cup of despair, but the chalice of opportunity. So let us seize it, not in fear, but in gladness - and, "riders on the earth together," let us go forward, firm in our faith, steadfast in our purpose, cautious of the dangers; but sustained by our confidence in the will of God and the promise of man.

RICHARD MILHOUS NIXON
SECOND INAUGURAL ADDRESS
SATURDAY, JANUARY 20, 1973

Although the Democratic Party maintained majorities in the Congress, the presidential ambitions of South Dakota Senator George McGovern were unsuccessful, with McGovern obtaining only 37% of the popular vote and 3% of the electoral vote.

...We have the chance today to do more than ever before in our history to make life better in America - to ensure better education, better health, better housing, better transportation, a cleaner environment - to restore respect for law, to make our communities more livable - and to insure the God-given right of every American to full and equal opportunity...

...We are embarking here today on an era that presents challenges great as those any nation, or any generation, has ever faced.

We shall answer to God, to history, and to our conscience for the way in which we use these years...

...Today, I ask your prayers that in the years ahead I may have God's help in making decisions that are right for America, and I pray for your help so that together we may be worthy of our challenge...

...Let us go forward from here confident in hope, strong in our faith in one another, sustained by our faith in God who created us, and striving always to serve His purpose.

GERALD RUDOLPH FORD, JR.
(Republican) Thirty-eighth President

b. July14, 1913, Omaha, Neb., birth name was Leslie Lynch King, jr.

d.

m. 1948, Elizabeth "Betty" Bloomer Warren; three sons, one daughter.

Father: Leslie L. King, Sr., his natural father, a wool dealer. Parents divorced when he was 2.

Gerald R. Ford, Sr., his step-father, a paint salesman. Married his mother when he was 3 and gave him his name.

Prep School: South High.

College: University of Michigan (worked year-round to support himself while playing football). He turned down pro-football offers to join the athletic staff of Yale University, and graduated from Yale Law School.

Profession: Dishwasher; football and boxing coach; seasonal Yellowstone Park ranger; co-owner of modeling agency; fashion model; lawyer; 13 term U. S. Representative; Vice President.

Military: Enlisted in Navy as an ensign; ended as a Lt. Comdr.

Denomination: Attended Episcopal Churches from boyhood on.

President from: August 9, 1974 to January 20, 1977.

Inaugurated at: East Room of the White House.

Sworn in by: Chief Justice Warren Burger.

Noteworthy: Ford is the only Chief Executive to not be elected either as Vice President or President. For the first four months of his presidency, Mr. Ford had no vice president. On December 19, 1974, Nelson Aldrich Rockefeller was sworn in as the 41st vice president of the United States, the second vice president in little more than a year to come to office through the recently enacted 25th Amendment.

Two assasination attempts were made on his life: one by Lynette Alice "Squeaky" Fromme, a Manson cult follower, and the other by Sara Jane Moore, a radical anti-government protestor. Ford was unhurt in both attempts and both women were sentenced to life imprisonment.

No Inaugural Address.

JAMES EARL ("JIMMY") CARTER, JR.
(Democrat) Thirty-ninth President

b. Oct. 1, 1924, at Plains, Georgia.
d.
m. 1946, Rosalyn Smith; three sons, one daughter.
Father: James Earl Carter, Sr., farmer; storekeeper; state legislator.
Prep School: Public schools.
College: Attended Georgia Southwestern College for one year; transferred to Georgia Institute of Technology as a naval ROTC student; transferred again and graduated from the United States Naval Academy, ranking 59th in a class of 820. Post graduate studies in nuclear physics at Union College.
Profession: U.S. Naval officer; agri-business owner; 2 term State Senator; Governor of Georgia, one term.
Military: Graduated from United States Naval Academy as an ensign, served seven years and ended service as a Lt.
Denomination: Southern Baptist.
Church Service: Deacon and Sunday School teacher at Plains Baptist Church; Bible class teacher at First Baptist Church in Washington while President; Volunteer work for Habitat for Humanity.
President from: January 20, 1977 to January 20, 1981.
Inaugurated at: The East Front of the Capitol.
Sworn in by: Chief Justice Warren Burger.
Bible used: The same Bible used in the first inauguration by George Washington and also one his mother had given to him.
Noteworthy: Surprised spectators after his inauguration by walking down Pennsylvania Avenue to the White House rather than riding in the limousine prepared for him.

JAMES EARL "JIMMY" CARTER
INAUGURAL ADDRESS
THURSDAY, JANUARY 20, 1977

The Democrats reclaimed the White House in the 1976 election.
The oath of office was again taken on the Bible used in the first inaugu-
ration by George Washington together with the Bible his mother had
given to him. The new President and his family surprised the spectators
by walking from the Capitol to the White House after the ceremony.

...As my high school teacher, Miss Julia Coleman, used to say:
"We must adjust to changing times and still hold to unchanging principles."

Here before me is the Bible used in the inauguration of our first
President, in 1789, and I have just taken the oath of office on the Bible my
mother gave me a few years ago, opened to a a timeless admonition from
the ancient prophet Micah:

"He hath showed thee, O man, what is good; and what doth the
Lord require of thee, but to do justly, and to love mercy, and to walk
humbly with thy God." (Micah 6:8)

...Ours was the first society openly to define itself in terms of
both spirituality and of human liberty. It is that unique self-definition
which has given us an exceptional appeal, but it also imposes on us a special obligation, to take on those moral duties which, when assumed, seem
invariably to be in our own best interests...

...Within us, the people of the United States, there is evident a
serious and purposeful rekindling of confidence. And I join in the hope
that when my time as your President has ended, people might say this
about our Nation: -that we had remembered the words of Micah and
renewed our search for humility, mercy, and justice...

RONALD WILSON REAGAN
(Republican) Fortieth President

b. Feb. 6, 1911, in Tampico, Illinois.

d.

m. Jane Wyman, one son, one daughter. Divorced.

m. 1952, Anne Frances "Nancy" Robbins Davis Reagan, one son, one daughter.

Father: John Edward Reagan, shop clerk and merchant.

Prep School: Public schools.

College: Eureka College, Eureka, Illinois.

Profession: Sports announcer; broadcaster; screen actor; president of the labor union, Screen Actors Guild; Governor of California.

Military: Capt., U.S. Army Air Corps during WWII.

Denomination: Disciples of Christ.

President from: January 20, 1981 to January 20, 1989.

First Term Inauguration: at the West Front of the Capitol for the first time.

Sworn in by: Chief Justice Warren Burger.

Second term inauguration: January 20th was a Sunday, and Reagan took the oath in the Grand Foyer of the White House, sworn in by Chief Justice Warren Burger.

January 21, 1985, the temperature was near zero and many inaugural events were canceled. President Reagan was the first President to be inaugurated in the Capitol Rotunda.

RONALD REAGAN
FIRST INAUGURAL ADDRESS
TUESDAY, JANUARY 20, 1981

For the first time, an inauguration ceremony was held on the ter-race of the West Front of the Capitol. In the election of 1980, the Republicans won the White House and a majority in the Senate. On inau-guration day, 52 American hostages held 444 days by the revolutionary government of Iran were released.

...Your dreams, your hopes, your goals are going to be the dreams, the hopes, and the goals of this administration, so help me God...

...I am told that tens of thousands of prayer meetings are being held on this day, and for that I am deeply grateful. We are a nation under God, and I believe God intended for us to be free. It would be fitting and good, I think, if on each Inauguration Day in future years it should be declared a day of prayer...

The crisis we are facing today...does require, however, our best effort, and our willingness to believe in ourselves and to believe in our capacity to perform great deeds; to believe that together, with God's help, we can and will resolve the problems which now confront us.

And, after all, why shouldn't we believe that? We are Americans. God bless you, and thank you.

RONALD REAGAN
SECOND INAUGURAL ADDRESS
MONDAY, JANUARY 21, 1985

January 20th was a Sunday, and the President took his second oath of office, administered by Chief Justice Warren Burger, in the Grand Foyer of the White House. Weather that hovered near zero that night and on Monday forced the planners to cancel many of the outdoor events for the second inauguration. For the first time a President took the oath of office in the Capitol Rotunda.

This day has been made brighter with the presence here of one who, for a time has been absent - Senator John Stennis.

God bless you and welcome back.

There is, however, one who is not with us today: Representative Gillis Long of Louisiana left us last night. I wonder if we could all join in a moment of silent prayer. (Moment of silent Prayer.) Amen.

This is, as Senator Mathias told us, the 50th time that we the people have celebrated this historic occasion. When the first President, George Washington, placed his hand upon the Bible, he stood less than a single day's journey by horseback from raw, untamed wilderness. So much has changed. And yet we stand together as we did two centuries ago.

...Well, with heart and hand, let us stand as one today: One people under God determined that our future shall be worthy of our past...

The time has come for a new American emancipation - a great national drive to tear down economic barriers and liberate the spirit of enterprise in the most distressed areas of our country. My friends, together we can do this, and do it we must, so help me God.

As an older American, I remember a time when people of different race, creed, or ethnic origin in our land found hatred and prejudice installed in social custom and, yes, in law. There is no story more heartening in our history than the progress that we have made toward the "brotherhood of man" that God intended for us. Let us resolve there will be no turning back or hesitation on the road to an America rich in dignity and abundant with opportunity for all our citizens.

For all our problems, our differences, we are together as of old, as we raise our voices to the God who is the Author of this most tender music. And may He continue to hold us close as we fill the world with our sound - sound in unity, affection, and love - one people under God, dedicated to the dream of freedom that He has placed in the human heart, called upon now to pass that dream on to a waiting and hopeful world.

...God bless you and may God bless America...

GEORGE HERBERT WALKER BUSH
(Republican) Forty-first President

b. June 12, 1924, in Milton, Massachusetts.
d.
m. 1945, Barbara Pierce Bush, 4 sons, 2 daughters.
Father: Prescott Bush, U.S. Senator from Connecticut.
Prep School: Greenwich Country Day School, Greenwich, Conn.; Phillips Academy, Andover, Mass.
College: Yale University.
Profession: Pilot; Oil Co. executive; U.S. Representative, two terms; Ambassador to U.N.; head of U.S. Liasion Office in Beijing; Director of CIA; Vice-President.
Military: U.S.N. pilot during WWII, earning the Distinguished Flying Cross and three Air Medals.
Denomination: Episcopalian. He and Mrs. Bush attend Sunday worship regularly, say their nightly prayers together, and do daily Bible readings.
Church Service: Vestryman at St. Anne's Episcopal Church, Kennebunkport, Maine.
President from: January 20, 1989 (The 200th Anniversary of the Presidency) to January 20, 1993.
Inaugurated at: The terrace of the West Front of the Capitol.
Sworn in by: Chief Justice William Rehnquist, on the Bible used by George Washington in 1789.
Noteworthy: When President Reagan vacated the White House on Inauguration Day, he left behind two handwritten notes for his former Vice President. The first was in the top drawer of the big mahogany desk in the Oval Office. It read: "George, don't let the turkeys get you down." The other note was found in a closet in the East Wing. It said, "George, keep the faith."

GEORGE BUSH
INAUGURAL ADDRESS
FRIDAY, JANUARY 20, 1989

The 200th anniversary of the Presidency was observed as George Bush took the executive oath on the same Bible George Washington used in 1789.

...I have just repeated word for word the oath taken by George Washington 200 years ago, and the Bible on which I placed my hand is the Bible on which he placed his...

...And my first act as President is a prayer. I ask you to bow your heads:

Heavenly Father, we bow our heads and thank You for Your love. Accept our thanks for the peace that yields this day and the shared faith that makes its continuance likely. Make us strong to do Your work, willing to heed and hear Your will, and write on our hearts these words: "Use power to help people." For we are given power not to advance our own purposes, nor to make a great show in the world, nor a name. There is but one just use of power, and it is to serve people. Help us to remember it, Lord. Amen...

...There is much to do; and tomorrow the work begins. I do not mistrust the future; I do not fear what is ahead. For our problems are large, but our heart is larger. Our challenges are great, but our will is greater. And if our flaws are endless, God's love is truly boundless.

Some see leadership as high drama, and the sound of trumpets calling, and sometimes it is that. But I see history as a book with many pages, and each day we fill a page with acts of hopefulness and meaning. The new breeze blows, a page turns, the story unfolds. And so today a chapter begins, a small and stately story of unity, diversity, and generosity - shared, and written, together.

Thank you. God bless you and God bless the United States of America.

WILLIAM JEFFERSON "BILL" CLINTON
(Democrat) Forty-second President

b. Aug. 19, 1946, in Hope, Ark. His birth name was William Jefferson Blythe, III (according to The World Almanac 1994), or William Jefferson Blythe, IV (according to The Worldbook Encyclopedia).

d.

m. 1975, Hillary Rodham Clinton, one daughter.

Father: William Jefferson Blythe, Jr., a traveling salesman who died in an accident before his son was born. At age 16, Bill Blythe changed his name to Bill Clinton, some years after his mother married Roger Clinton. (Worldbook says his name change was at age 15.)

Prep School: Attended Catholic school during the period of desegregation in Hot Springs, Ark., later attended public school.

College: Georgetown University; Oxford University; Yale Law School.

Military: None.

Profession: Campaign staff for George McGovern; staff member House Judiciary Committee; taught at University of Arkansas Law School; unsuccessful candidate for U.S. House of Representatives; Arkansas State Attorney General; 5 term Arkansas Governor.

Denomination: Southern Baptist, member of Immanuel Baptist Church, Little Rock, Arkansas, where he had often sung in the choir. In a 1992 interview he said "If I didn't believe in God, if I weren't in my view, a Christian, if I didn't believe ultimately in the perfection of life after death, my life would have been that much more difficult."

President from: January 20, 1993 to---

Inaugurated at: A platform built off of the terrace of the West Front of the Capitol.

Sworn in by: Chief Justice William Rehnquist.

Noteworthy: The Lesbian and Gay Bands of America marched in the Inaugural Parade and the Girl Scouts of America passed out American flags and AIDS awareness ribbons.

On July 12, 1995, in an address to school children at James Madison High School, President Clinton told the students about the Religious Freedom Restoration Act and told them signing the Act into law in 1993 was "one of the proudest things I've been able to do as President."

WILLIAM JEFFERSON " BILL" CLINTON
INAUGURAL ADDRESS
WEDNESDAY, JANUARY 20, 1993

A few days after President Clinton gave his 14 minute Inaugural Address, Gen. Colin Powell began letting it be known that he would resign as Chairman of the Joint Chiefs of Staff if Clinton lifted the ban on homosexuals in the military.

My fellow citizens:

Today we celebrate the mystery of American renewal.

This ceremony is held in the depth of winter. But, by the words we speak and the faces we show the world, we force the spring.

A spring reborn in the world's oldest democracy, that brings forth the vision and courage to reinvent America.

When our Founders boldly declared America's independence to the world and our purposes to the Almighty, they knew that America, to endure, would have to change.

Not change for changes's sake, but change to preserve America's ideals--life, liberty, the pursuit of happiness. Though we march to the music of our time, our mission is timeless.

Each generation of Americans must define what it means to be an American...

...Profound and powerful forces are shaking and remaking our world, and the urgent question of our time is whether we can make change our friend and not our enemy...

...Thomas Jefferson believed that to preserve the very foundations of our nation, we would need dramatic change from time to time. Well, my fellow citizens, this is our time. Let us embrace it...

...To renew America we must be bold...

...To renew America, we must revitalize our democracy...

...To renew America, we must meet challenges abroad as well at home...

But our greatest strength is the power of our ideas, which are still new in many lands. Across the world, we see them embraced - and we rejoice. Our hopes, our hearts, our hands are with those on every continent who are building democracy and freedom. Their cause is America's cause...

...and so, my fellow Americans, at the edge of the 21st century, let us begin with energy and hope, with faith and discipline, and let us work until our work is done. The Scripture says, "And let us not be weary in well-doing, for in due season, we shall reap, if we faint not."

From this joyful mountaintop of celebration, we hear a call to service in the valley. We have heard the trumpets. We have changed the guard. And now, each in our way, and with God's help, we must answer the call.

Thank you and God bless you all.

INTERESTING FACTS ABOUT THE PRESIDENTS

No Military Service
John Adams
Thomas Jefferson
James Madison
John Quicy Adams
Martin Van Buren
James Knox Polk
Millard Fillmore
Chester Alan Arthur
Grover Cleveland
William Howard Taft
Woodrow Wilson
Warren G. Harding
Calvin Coolidge
Herbert Clark Hoover
Franklin Delano Roosevelt
William Jefferson Clinton

Changed Names
Ulysses Simpson Grant
Grover Cleveland
Woodrow Wilson
Calvin Coolidge
Dwight David Eisenhower
Gerald R. Ford, jr.
William Jefferson Clinton

No Children
George Washington
James Madison
Andrew Jackson
James Knox Polk
James Buchanan
Warren G. Harding

No College
George Washington
Andrew Jackson
Martin Van Buren
Zachary Taylor
Millard Fillmore
Abraham Lincoln
Andrew Johnson
Grover Cleveland

Preacher's Kids
Chester Alan Arthur
Grover Cleveland
Woodrow Wilson
Herbert Hoover

Homeschooled
(in part or whole)
George Washington
Thomas Jefferson
James Madison
Andrew Jackson
William Henry Harrison
James Knox Polk
Zachary Taylor
Millard Fillmore*
Abraham Lincoln
Andrew Johnson*
Benjamin Harrison
Theodore Roosevelt
Woodrow Wilson
Franklin Roosevelt
*(hometaught as adults
by their wives)

BIBLIOGRAPHY

1. Barzman, Sol. The First Ladies, New York: Cowles Book Company, Inc., (1970).
2. Chronicle of America, Chronicle Publications, Mount Kisco, N.Y. (1989).
3. Clinton, William Jefferson. Inaugural Address, reprinted The Washington Post, January 21, 1993 p. A26.
4. DeGregorio, William A., The Complete Book of U.S. Presidents: From George Washington to Bill Clinton, Wings Books, New York (1993).
5. Eidsmoe, John. Christianity and the Constitution, Grand Rapid, Michigan: Baker Book House (1987).
6. Famighetti, Robert. The World Book Encyclopedia (1994), Mahwah, New Jersey (1994).
7. Federer, William J., America's God and Country, Encyclopedia of Quotations, FAME Publishing, Inc.(1994).
8. Ferris, Robert G., James H. Charleton, Asst. Ed., The Presidents, United States Department of the Interior National Park Service, Rev. Ed. (1977).
9. Halstead, Murak. The Illustrious Life of William McKinley, (1901).
10. Harper's, v. 289, p.6 July 1994.
11. Haskin, Frederic J., Presidents and Their Wives The Haskin Information Service, Washington, D.C. (1935).
12. Hillman, William. Mr. President: The First Publication From the Personal Diaries, Private Letters Papers and Revealing Interviews of Harry S Truman, Farrar, Straus and Young, New York (1952).
13. Joint Congressional Committee on Inaugural Ceremonies. Inaugural Addresses of the Presidents of the United States, Washington, D.C. U.S. Government Printing Office, Bicentennial Ed., (1989).
14. The 1989 Information Please Almanac, Boston: Houghton Mifflin Company (1989).
15. LaHaye, Tim. Faith of Our Founding Fathers, Brentwood, Tennessee, Woglemuth & Hyatt, Publishers, Inc. (1989).
16. Newsweek, v.123, May 2, 1994.
17. Roche, O.I.A., Ed. The Jefferson Bible: With the Annotated Commentaries on Religion of Thomas Jefferson, Clarkson N. Potter, Inc., New York (1964).
18. Time, v. 141, Feb. 1, 1993.
19. Tyler, Moses Coit. Patrick Henry, Houghton, Mifflin and Company, Boston and New York (1895).
20. U.S. News & World Report, v. 114, Feb. 1, 1993.
21. U.S. News & World Report, V. 116, May 2, 1994.
22. White, William Allen. Woodrow Wilson, Boston & New York: Houghton Mifflin Company (1925).
23. Wilson, Fred Taylor. Pen Pictures of the Presidents, Nashville, Tennessee: Southwestern Company (1937).
24. The World Almanac and Book of Facts 1994. Funk & Wagnalls (1994).

VICTORIES!

IN THE BATTLE FOR AMERICA

Published Monthly by
Attorney at Law
J. Michael Sharman
114 N. West Street
Culpeper, Virginia 22701
1(540)825-9600
Subscription Rate $20 per year

Are you sick and tired of hearing bad news?

My work as a Christian attorney has allowed me to see that there is very definitely a battle going on for the soul of America which is being fought out in our courtrooms, legislatures, and voting booths. This is probably not news to you, like me you are probably all too aware of the many negative trends in the country today. What is noteworthy, however, is that Christian "soldiers" are victorious in many of these battles -- and we never hear of those victories. Too often we pass around the stories of defeats like so much blank ammo when what we really need to do is to hand out the live ammunition which is the reports of the many victories in the battle for America. These are just a few of those reports:

Christian students do have a right to student activity fees to publish their Christian publications, Rosenberger v. University of Virginia.

Christian ministries do have a right to speak out on political issues and about political candidates, Federal Election Commission v. Christian Action Network.

A private employer does have a right to fire an employee simply because he is homosexual, DeMuth v. Miller.

Abortionists can be convicted of murder for their conduct during abortions, State v. David Benjamin.

Judges can display the Ten Commandments and pray in their courtrooms, Freedom From Religion Foundation v. Moore.

Evangelists do have the right to preach on a street corner without a license, Anderson v. City of Cleburne.

Veterans can exclude homosexuals from their parade, Hurley v. Irish-American Gay, Lesbian and Bisexual Group of Boston.

The **Victories!** journal which is published monthly is an attempt to inform God's people about these successes and the many other good news stories that are regularly occurring.

Why not take this opportunity to subscribe and be informed and encouraged today?

Send $20.00 with each new subscription to **Victories!** 114 N. West Street, Culpeper, VA 22701

Name _____   Name _____

Street _____   Street _____

City _____ Zip_____   City _____ Zip_____

VCTRYPG.DOC 20